THE AMERICAN

ONE-ROOM SCHOOLHOUSE

BY

HENRY J. KAUFFMAN

The American One-Room Schoolhouse

Copyright © 1997

COVER

*The Miller one-room elementary school
located ten miles west of York, Pennsylvania, along Route 30.*
Courtesy: Dr. Mary Hallman.

Library of Congress Number: 97-74130

International Standard Book Number: 1-883294-54-1

Reprinted 2005 by
Masthof Press
*R. R. 1, Box 20, Mill Road
Morgantown, PA 19543*

Contents

1. Introduction 1

2. Early Starts 6

3. Nineteenth-Century Idealism 13

4. Amish One-Room Schoolhouses 24

5. The Teacher 29

6. School Books 39

7. Teaching Apparatus 57

8. Desks and Chairs 64

9. Rules and Regulations 67

Two one-room school buildings located in Washington Boro, Lancaster County, Pennsylvania. When one building became crowded, a second one was built adjoining it.

The McGuffey School at Dearborn, Michigan, is typical of the early one-room schoolhouses.
Courtesy: Henry Ford Museum and Greenfield Village.

∼≫ 1 ≪∼

Introduction

It is probably a fallacy to equate education with the number of years spent within the halls of a schoolhouse, particularly when the school year varies from several weeks to several months. Students who spend eight, ten, or twelve years in school find that they are not prepared for potential employment, nor for the solution of life's knotty problems.

After the writer has read much that has been written about education in the eighteenth and nineteenth centuries, he must admit that somewhere in those times existed a secret formula which is not readily seen. How did a broken down schoolhouse which sheltered a poorly trained teacher and a gang of rebellious youths

produce the America we know today? It is certainly obvious that the "rank and file" achieved on a level not possible with all the yellow buses and the commodious places available in all parts of the country. The one-room schoolhouse has disappeared in the most poorly settled parts of the country, and Johnny and Mary are still unable to the manage the three "Rs."

One might hope that a meticulous study of the past will reveal its mystery, but unfortunately, after the present writer has made his effort, the puzzle still remains.

Today, businessmen and parents are deploring the fact that Johnny and Mary cannot skillfully manipulate the three "Rs." They con-

1

It was customary for photographers to travel the countryside and take photographs of complete schools. Students were grouped outside the building as in this photograph at Locust Grove Elementary School about 1913. The author is not on this photograph, but his sister and brother are. Students are wearing the typical dress used in the countryside at the time of this picture.

tend that this deficiency can be laid at the doorstep of our modern school. These institutions, they charge, are plagued by "education" therapists who introduce new untried concepts to replace earlier successful ones to prepare our youths for life's journey. There are all sorts of so-called frills—so goes the education—to divert time and effort which should be concentrated on learning to read and write. Home and business knows that although George Washington had very little formal schooling, somehow he learned to become a surveyor, a general, and President of the United States. Examples of his penmanship show that he not only had the basic skill of writing, but that he could also compose elegant and incisive phrases which made his writing attractive and useful. And, somewhere he certainly learned to add, subtract, multiply, and divide.

An early philosopher of education commented that after a person had learned to read and write, the rest of his education lay within himself. Although such a concept was not the goal of education in a one-room schoolhouse, it does appear to have been their function.

An author who proposes to write about the one-room schoolhouse should perhaps have attended one himself and should enjoy the nostalgia of describing some of his experiences in such a building. Although a student six years of age would have had little experience in making appraisals, my best recollections are that life in that school was very pleasant, and I was eager to attend. The teacher, whose name was Carrie Ligget, was a warm, affectionate woman who rarely raised her voice. She was quite opposite to the vicious females who reputedly "kept school" in those good old days. She had complete control of the room with her soft speech and charming manner. There was little competition among students, and all seemed grateful for the opportunity to meet as a group and study together. I suspect our elders had a hand in helping to create that atmosphere.

I was born in York County, Pennsylvania, in 1908, and at the age of six entered the first grade in Locust Grove Elementary School. Classes were held there from grades one through eight; grades nine to twelve met in a senior high school. I was only the fourth person from that school to go to high school and college.

I have virtually no memories of experiences in the first grade. Although I don't remember it, I know that I must have been vaccinated before the first day of school. I remember my later years with considerable pleasure. One of my less serious problems was to get my feet back into shoes after walking barefooted all summer. Without shoes one's feet spread, but after a few days all seemed to go along normally. Sometime around the second or third grade I remember some special clothing I wore the first day. My real pride was a white shirt made by my Aunt Lydia, with whom I lived, my mother having died when I was three years old. My weekday attire was usually a blue or dark-colored shirt, and I prized my white one very highly. Of course, like most of the other scholars, I had a new pair of shoes.

I remember that I had only a few books in the early grades, about which my aunt frequently commented, for when she went briefly to school her few books had to be supplied by her parents. In her day most of the students had different books for reading and other subjects, so teaching became very difficult.

In those days all the students had to walk to school, regardless of the distance. From an introspective point of view, this could be regarded as a fine way of getting a little exercise. The teacher also walked. In the winter the walking became very difficult in deep snow, but I don't recall of a day ever being missed because of the weather.

School sessions started about 8:30 a.m. when children were summoned from the school yard by ringing a cast iron bell hung in a cupola on the roof of the schoolhouse. On very rare occasions a student was allowed to ring the bell by pulling a rope on the floor level. Such an opportunity was regarded as an honor by the rest of the students. Upon entering the building, the pupils hung their wraps on wooden pegs near the entry, removed their overshoes, and placed their lunches on a broad shelf installed for that purpose. Later we got desks with a shelf for books and lunches.

After all the students were quietly in their seats, opening exercises were conducted by the teacher. She read an excerpt from the Bible and led the group in repeating the Lord's Prayer. There was no Pledge of Allegiance at that time. As a matter of fact, such a sentiment was not needed to enlist the patriotism of the students. There were no protests from parents or students to this procedure. Announcements were made, after which the young learners turned immediately to their lessons. They were seated according to their size, the smaller ones in front near the teacher's desk, the larger ones in the rear.

Classes had different numbers of enrollees—at times, perhaps, only one, two, or three; others as many as twelve. The higher grades were usually smaller, for when students became old enough to quit school, many of them did. Such students, with their parents, obviously placed little importance on a thorough elementary education.

The daily routine began with the teacher calling a particular grade to the front of the room to sit on a long bench, occupied only when a class was reciting. Classes in spelling and mental arithmetic stood at the bench; in reading, geography, and history they sat. A class in arithmetic "worked" their problems on the blackboard.

Not all grades and classes recited every day, but the schedule was staggered so that each class had two or three recitations each week. I looked forward to recitation in some classes; others I was only an unwilling participant. The teacher regarded reading as the most important class in the curriculum, and I was a good "reader." Being a good reader was judged as a sign of high intelligence and high achievement in all the classes.

While one class was reciting, others sat at their desks studying the lessons which would be called for later in the day. But concentration was almost impossible, for there always seemed to be distractions.

As students passed from their desks to the front of the room, they sometimes used the occasion to punch another student whom they disliked, or just as a joke. Such action could, of course, not be tolerated, and if the teacher saw the action, the offender was penalized by only a scolding. If such action was constantly repeated, the penalty was to write, "I will behave properly," 500 times during the recess period. This was a very distasteful and humbling experience, for all the students knew about it. However, the cure was not always effective. An incident in modern life relates to this activity. A judge in a traffic court found a teacher in front of him. Instead of leveling a monetary fine, he ordered that she write, "Speeding is dangerous," 500 times.

At mid-morning, there was a ten-to-fifteen-minute recess period when all the students went into the school yard for exercise and fresh air. If a student was physically handicapped and could not run and play, he was required to walk in the schoolroom, or at least get some physical activity to make sitting a bit easier. The after-

The interior of the schoolhouse reflected the daily school life of the nineteenth century. Two circles of pupils' desks, a teacher's desk, a central pot-bellied stove, textbooks, and other instructional helps capture the earlier use. Courtesy: Delaware Division of Historical and Cultural Affairs.

noon session was similar, with a recess in the middle and dismissal at 3:30 p.m.

No fence dividing the school yard between boys and girls was recommended by early school planners. On rare occasions the teacher came out to watch or participate in the games. This act was highly thought of by the students. Recess was terminated by the ringing of the bell, whereupon all the scholars entered the building for further study and recitations. About a half hour was assigned for eating lunch, but because I lived nearby, I went home for that meal. It was usually very simple, often consisting of only a bowl of soup and some crackers. At lunch most of the students took a drink of water from a common dipper which hung on the side of a bucket. My school had no well, so scholars volunteered to go for a bucket of water at my home site. The well was located about 100 feet from the house, over which a giant willow tree grew.

Geography was not taught until the fifth or sixth grade. The lessons consisted mainly of memorizing the names of the state of the nation, and later the nations of the world, as well as their capitals and most important cities. I had a good memory and excelled in this work. Different subjects were enumerated on the report cards, and I always got an "A" in geography. History lessons were also principally a matter of memory, and I also got an "A" in that subject. Mathematics was drill work with students solving problems on a piece of paper and handing them to the teacher, who corrected them. This was followed by each scholar doing new problems on the blackboard. If students had been habitually copying their work at their seats from a cooperating neighbor, this act would be discovered by his inability to solve problems at the blackboard.

It was previously mentioned that the spelling class did not sit on the "recitation" bench. They lined up alphabetically at first (in the old times, along a crack in the floor) and the person at the head of the class was given a word to spell. If he was unable to spell the word correctly, it was given to the second person. If he spelled it correctly he went to the head of the class. This procedure continued throughout the lesson, the smart ones eventually standing at the head of the class, the dull ones at the bottom. Though this was a standard procedure in all schools, our teacher was very careful not to humiliate children at the bottom of the class. They were encouraged and told to study harder so they would stand higher another time. Miss Ligget was always kind in her relations with the students.

The most disliked lessons were in physiology, a study of bones and other parts of the anatomy. Some schools had a skull, and the most modern ones had a skeleton to illustrate parts of the body, but my school had neither. We were not told the importance of this subject, but I am sure we would not have liked it better anyway.

During certain times the whole school participated in activities led by the teacher. One exercise was penmanship (slightly disliked), when students copied letters or words printed at the top of the "copy" books. At other times all the students sang together. Many schools were equipped with an organ, a great asset if the teacher could play it. The repertoire included semi-popular songs and always included a hymn.

In art periods students were issued special paper to copy a drawing made by the teacher on the blackboard, or a poster advertising commodities used in the home. The best renderings were hung on a string across the top of the blackboard or along a side wall. In the early twentieth-century wax crayons were issued to pupils to color the line drawings made. The young artists were often inclined to waste crayons for other purposes, for which they were reprimanded, or possibly even denied crayons by the teacher until better care was given them.

Sometimes regular school work was dropped for a special entertainment, which consisted of learning poems or putting on a play appropriate for the season. On very special occasions parents were invited to attend these affairs. Naturally, some of the young thespians were very nervous when appearing alone before a school audience; others had poise and did very well.

It might also be reported that some unscheduled activity occurred at a one-room schoolhouse. I can definitely recall that one year at Halloween, a number of us visited the school and placed a large number of corn shocks from an adjacent field around the front door. This procedure was made more secure by placing some rails from a nearby rail fence among the corn shocks. To top off the situation, one of the group crawled up to the bell tower and tied the clapper fast so the bell would not ring. These acts were a curious way to express our affection for the teacher, but that was the sole motivation.

Of course, the next morning the teacher was unable to enter the school and she had to wait until some boys arrived to remove the corn shocks and rails. And, of course, they were the very same ones who placed them there the night before. In a triumphant mood the teacher entered the room, but when she went to ring the bell, there was no sound. Again, the same boy who tied the clapper went up to untie it, and all was back in working order. These little experiences made life a bit more interesting for a school day, and I will remember them for a very long time.

Finally, I must come to an incident of major importance, but one that had to be tolerated. The trend began toward the hiring of male teachers, and I had one the last two years of my career. I will not mention the name of the man for he was very unpopular. He was a very stern man, and one day he brought a bundle of sticks about a yard long and an inch in diameter. He proudly displayed them to the students and then put them high on a shelf where they could not be reached. I saw most of those sticks broken into pieces on my classmates; fortunately, I never felt them. This man's manner and methods were in sharp contrast to Miss Ligget's, so only a few apples were brought to his desk! There is some uncertainty about an improvement being made in the conduct of a one-room school.

My final experience in the one-room schoolhouse was to take an eighth-grade examination. Passing it was required to qualify for enrollment in senior high school. There was no preparation for it; however, most of the students passed, including myself. My life in a one-room school was doubtless one of the happiest periods of my life. I cannot say my learning was erudite, but it prepared me for what lay ahead, and that was its function.

Something seems to have occurred beyond the passing of grades and the assigning of marks. Factors like self-reliance, honesty, and the persistent stretching toward a goal fitted me well to survive and solve many of life's problems. I would love to shake the hand of Carrie Ligget and tell her how positively she influenced my life.

2

Early Starts

Our distance from the beginning of formal education in America is so great that one rarely hears about early starts on this side of the Atlantic. Schools did exist in Europe before the first settlers arrived here, and they set a precedent for the establishment of schools in America. It is not likely that the American institutions assumed the same form as those in Europe, and the development is different; however, it is a fact that the seed was planted there and subsequent growth occurred here.

In 1642, twelve years after the settlement of Boston, the General Court of Massachusetts mandated that parents or guardians be responsible for the training (education) of their children. Select men were appointed or elected to see that children could read the Bible, and also beset to some "useful work." It is very obvious that a need was felt for the children to read the Bible, and that was also the goal for schools in other settlements. Just when the apprentice system was started to train boys to become professional craftsmen is not known; however, skilled craftsmen were arriving in America with experience in the trades, and they soon followed the European system of training apprentices. Such activity was important for the survival for social and economic conditions. As a matter of fact, it might have been more important than learning to read the Bible. It might be mentioned also that one of the injunctions to the masters was to see that his apprentice learned to read the Bible.

In a comment about these early times, a statement appears in *Old Time School and School Books*, by Clifton Johnson that:

It being one chief aim of the "ould deluder Sathan," to keep men from a knowledge of the Scriptures, effort must be made to thwart that "ould deluder" that learning may not be buried in the grave of fathers in the church and commonwealth.

It was therefore ordered that any community consisting of fifty households shall see that all children be taught to write and read, the wages of a teacher to be paid by the parents of the students, or by town support. These matters relate to the starting of elementary schools. After the child could read and write, he went on to a grammar school where he was taught fundamentals of Latin and Greek. From there he went to a university; Harvard was established in 1736. The legislature of Connecticut soon followed with similar laws as did lawful bodies in other states such as New York and Pennsylvania.

The earliest Dutch school was formed in Manhattan in 1633 with Adam Roelansen as its master. This school was sponsored by the Dutch Church and has been in operation as late as 1886. Education was of such importance to members of the congregation that in their marriage ceremony the participants had to promise to bring their children up in a civilized way, which included sending them to school or otherwise having them to learn to read, write, and "cypher."

Early suggestions were made in regard to education in Pennsylvania. In one of the early mandates for the embryonic state, William Penn said:

That, therefore, which makes a good constitution must keep it, viz: men of wisdom and virtue, qualities that because they descend not with worldly inheritance, must be carefully propagated by virtue of the education of youth, for which ages will owe more to the care and prudence of founders, and successive magistry, than to their parents for their private patrimonies. [1682]

Although the data about early starts in education in Virginia are not easily available, the enlightened stature of the adults of the region suggest that some early plans were made. Much publicity has been given to the tutors and "field schools" of Virginia; research on the subject of education does reveal the true state of affairs.

Although New England and Virginia were both English colonies, the one-room school situation was different in the two regions. Both were organized on the English parish system, but unlike New England, conditions in Virginia did not support a one-room school plan for a number of reasons. First, there were only a few towns in Virginia; the families were not very close knit; and most of the settlers were not on one economic level.

The situation about one-room schools is described in *Parish Education In Virginia*, by Guy Fred Wells, New York, 1969.

It was not the custom of parishes of colonial Virginia to provide schoolhouses for the free use of the master to induce them to conduct schools. The only case mentioned on record of the Linhaven Parish, Princess Anne County. In the minutes of the vestry meeting on March 2, 1736, the following entry appears.

On the motion of Col. Anthony Walke that the old church woo'd be a convenient place to make a public school off for instructing children to learning, that liberty might be given for ye applying to that purpose, ye vestry taking said proposal also being of the opinion that after it is made commodious 'twould be an encouragement to induce a master constantly to attend thereon Do therefore unanimously Resolve that ye said church be, and it is hereby given for the use aforesaid, and to and for no other use or purpose whatever.

Another rare example is cited as follows:

At a court held for Essex Co. Feb. 10, 1704. On motion of Capt. Robert Coleman, it is considered by the Court that the old Prison standing at Hobbes Hole Tappahannock be appropriated for the use of a schoolhouse is referred to the consideration of the next Court.

Thus, it is clear that with a few exceptions the parishes of Virginia did not aid in the education of children by establishing free schools, furnishing school buildings, nor for paying for instruction in private (parish) schools. There were, however, many examples of endowed schools which were not supported by public funds.

There is a record of endowed free schools being open to all students, the earliest reference of a school starting in 1634-35. A man named Syms gave 200 acres of land in the parish of Elizabeth City, together with the milk and increase of eight cows. The school to be maintained for a learned and honest man (teacher) to keep upon the described ground a free school for the instruction of pupils. It was further declared that the authorities of Elizabeth City to see that all demands were met; and, when there was an increase in cattle, a schoolhouse be built and the excess applied for the educating of poor children, "or decayed or maimed persons."

In 1647 it was recognized that there was the original 200 acres, forty milk cows, and other accommodations which deserve perpetual memory. In the court records of 1693, there is evidence that the school continued in operation. It was ordered that:

Robert Crook, Schoolmaster, of Symmes school be allowed and paid for his charges in repairing ye school House two old cows in lieu thereof.

Although the endowed free schools were open to all of the children, they were not particularly successful. The wide distribution of the families kept many students from attending, as well as a marked disinterest in education by the poorest families. To this might be added some disinterest on the part of the trustees in keeping them up and seeing that they were supplied with a proper teacher.

In the wills of the men who endowed the free schools it was only mentioned that child-ren should be taught. However, the fact that female apprentices were to have an education suggested that girls also attended free schools. All persons were required to take apprentices who might logically use them; the custom had some success only because a fine was imposed for refusal.

Little formal activity occurred in the interest of public education in Virginia until after the Revolution. And, not until December 22, 1796, was a public school law passed by the Virginia legislature. The vital part of this mandate follows:

At every one of these schools shall be taught reading, writing, and common arithmetic; and all the free children, male and female, resident within the respective sections, shall be entitled to receive tuition gratis, for the term of three years, and as much longer at their private expense, as their parents, guardians, or friends think proper. The said aldermen shall from time to time appoint a teacher to each school, and shall remove him as they see cause.

They, or some of them, shall visit every school once in every half year, at least, examine the scholars, and superintend the conduct of the teachers in everything relative to the school.

The salary of the teacher with the expense of building and repairing a schoolhouse in each section shall be defrayed by the inhabitants of each county in proportion to the amount of their assessments and county levies, to be ascertained by the altermen of each county respectively, and shall be collected by the sheriff of each county.

In 1809 it was known that the courts had discretionary power in enforcing the law, and it was reported that in no instance was the law complied with. Problems like a fear of higher taxes, a long distance for the children to walk to school, and the usurping of the parental prerogative nullified the good intent of the law.

Knowing how slow corporate bodies move, it seems reasonable to decide that despite a commitment toward education, buildings were not built "overnight" in any of the geographical areas. There was little national pride in many important matters until after the Revolution, but there is evidence for the support for erection of buildings after 1776.

The modes of construction used in different geographical regions was followed in building schoolhouses. Pit saws and sawmills were operating in New England which caused their buildings to be covered with clapboards. The common use of logs was followed in Pennsylvania, not only in the eighteenth century, but well into the nineteenth. Because Virginia was an English colony, it seems reasonable to expect that their buildings were also covered with clapboards.

To be more specific about school buildings, most of them were rectangular in shape, with a wide variation in size. One commentator points out that the major motive in building schoolhouses seems to have been an attempt to see how small a building could be built to accommodate the largest number of students. It was not uncommon to have as many as sixty to a hundred pupils in a building, and very few were a size to comfortably accommodate that many students.

Although having basically similar characteristics, schools came into being by different routes. Some of the earliest schools began operating in a family residence. Presumably, the occupant of the house was the teacher, although not necessarily so. Such a room, appropriately furnished and open to the public, can be seen at the Nathan Hale homestead at Coventry, Connecticut. Although this is not a one-room schoolhouse, it did operate in one room, which permits its mention in this survey. There is a chance, of course, that schoolrooms of this type were better cared for and more comfortable than the single one-room edifice.

Schools in homes would seem to be the logical way to operate "moving schools." They were instituted to function in different parts of a large community, so that all students would be within a comfortable walking distance to their schools. These classrooms moved two or three times during a school year.

Another mode for starting a school was to use the village church, or meetinghouse, as was the custom in New England. In a time when buildings were at a premium, it was a very logical procedure to use a building seven days a week: on Sunday for religious services, the rest of the week for school. And, of course, for town meetings when they did not interfere with church or school activities.

Such scheduling was a very natural one, and convenient, for sometimes the minister served also as a teacher, or the teacher performed duties in the church. It is pointed out in *Eighteenth Century Reformed Church Schools*, by Fredrick George Livingood, 1930.

Among the neglected self sacrificing heroes of colonial history, none deserve more credit than the school teachers. Not among the least of those who also served was the German parochial schoolmaster. Upon him fell the maintenance of church and school in many places. In addition to keeping school he was expected to act as organist and chorister, and in the absence of the minister he was expected to read sermons and conduct public worship.... Had it not been for these parochial schoolmasters the work of the church would have suffered seriously, and without their services many colonial youths would have even more limited education, limited as it was under the best circumstances.

Outstanding work in the education of their youths was carried on by the Moravians in America. Again, their students were taught in a single room which was part of a larger building; nevertheless, it was done in one room. James Pyle Wickersham describes the situation with the Moravians in his *History Of Education In Pennsylvania.*

Parents placed their children in the Nurseries at the age of one to two years, and here they were fed and clothed, instructed and cared for at common expense, and by officers selected to perform these duties by the congregation. When a child arrived at a certain age he was transferred to a higher department called the "Boarding School," and there received further instruction suited to his requirements. This plan of bringing up children, whatever objections may be made to it on other accounts, was admirably calculated to develop talent for teaching, and to evolve sound principles and correct methods of instruction.

The famous pioneer in educational philosophy, named Comenius, was a Moravian teacher before he became a preacher. A number of his writings helped to lay the foundation of teaching methods in his day. The schools of the Moravians were at first started for Moravians only, but they were so successful that outsiders applied for admission, which was frequently granted. Other church groups who operated schools were the Reformed, Lutherans, Baptists, Presbyterians, Friends, and Catholics. Of course, schools existing today are sponsored by religious groups, the most numerous being those of the Catholics.

Another popular action in the early years of settlement was the establishment of schools by a cross-section of religious faiths. These people came to see that there was virtue in combining sectarian interests in one school and formed what has been called "neighborhood," "pay," or "subscription" schools. To create these a "town meeting" was called and a committee formed to look into matters relating to the starting and continuing operation of a school. This body of men is duplicated in the twentieth century by organizations known as "school boards."

Another type of instruction was available in a one-room school building in the southern states, where a wealthy planter chose to educate his children instead of sending them to England. He organized a school and hired a teacher for his own family. However, this arrangement was soon thrown open to nearby families also, who sent their children and thus helped to pay the expense of operating the school. They were called "field schools," for they were placed in a field which had lost its fertility for the growing of tobacco or other crops.

A mode of education following in the South that did not involve a special building was "putting out" children. Although this practice was not followed only by poor people, they were the principal participants. The child or children acted usually as servants in the household of a wealthy planter, their parents hoping that some of his knowledge and culture would "rub off" on the youngsters. The practice is described in *Virginians At Home*, by Edmund S. Morgan, 1952.

It was among the lower classes, however, that the practice of "putting out" children in other families was most common, and here the motives are not clear. Sometimes the family was too poor to support all its children, in which case both boys and girls might be bound out as apprentices in other families.

More often the motive was not directly economic—not, that is, to relieve the family of the burden of feeding and clothing the children, but educational. Children were placed in other families as apprentices, in order to learn a trade (in this case plantation management).

The first problem to be resolved in the erection of a school building was the selection of the site. Writers about school matters in the nineteenth century are very critical of the locations elected in the early times; however, that will be discussed at a later time in this study. It is probably that when a town was laid out in New England, a spot was allocated for the meetinghouse and/or a schoolhouse. Records show that the land for the schoolhouses were often gifts of individuals, especially the field schools of the South; and there is at least one record of such a donation in Pennsylvania. It is reported in the *Life And Works Of Christopher Dock*, by Martin G. Brumbaugh, Philadelphia and London, 1908.

By deed, dated June 8, 1717, Van Bebber conveyed to several trustees one hundred acres of ground, stipulating therein that "it shall be lawful for all and every need of the inhabitants of the above'd Bebber Township to build a school and fence in a sufficient burying place upon herein granted one hundred acres of land there to have their children and those respective families taught and instructed, and to bury their dead.

The schoolhouses built in the eighteenth century must have been of uneven quality. Certainly when a building was new, it was fairly "air tight" and attractive looking. Due to an uncertain commitment to education, some of these buildings might have become very shabby in a short time. Dr. Wickersham reports about early schoolhouses in Franklin County, Pennsylvania. Because Franklin County might have been considered "hinterland," conditions might have been a bit worse there than in the eastern section of the state.

The houses or cabins, used for school purposes, were of the simplest structure, being built of logs, or poles, and the space between them filled with chips of wood, and plastered with mortar made of clay. The boards on the roof were generally secured by heavy poles extending from one end to the other. The chimney was built of sticks of wood plastered and almost large enough to occupy one side of the house. The windows were not so extensive as the chimney, there being from three to four panes of glass in each, and about four of such in a building. The furniture was also of the simplest kind. It consisted of benches, made of logs split in two and hewn down to the proper thickness, supported by four legs. The stools and tables were made of the same material in a similar manner.

Dr. Wickersham comments about other log buildings in which one log from the west end was left out and covered with oiled paper to admit light. In others he observed that the construction was so faulty that snakes could crawl through the room, and often did. In still another description he points out that the floor was bare ground, which became very dusty when dry. Mischievous students sometimes kicked up the dirt with their bare feet, much to the consternation of the teacher.

The early schools consisted of a single room with a door and openings (windows). All were heated by a fireplace located in one of the short sides of the building. There is frequent mention of the lack of wood, or possibly a supply of green wood for the fireplace. In the winter the wood pile on the outside of the schoolhouse was often covered with snow, and wood had to be coaxed to burn. The classroom was cold when students arrived unless the teacher got there earlier and started the fire. Wood was supplied by the families of the students, some giving hard wood, other foul and rotten sticks. If a family were delinquent in supplying wood, their children could not sit near the fireplace until fuel was brought in. The larger students often gathered around the fireplace, barring the smaller ones from the warmth. It was not uncommon to hear a small student say to the teacher, "Please, may I come near the fire?" Of course, green wood produced smoke, and students often had to rub their eyes so they could see reasonably well.

When schoolhouses had a wooden floor it was usually a puncheon type, logs split in half with the smooth side up. In rare occasions, a theater-type floor was installed with the teacher's desk on the lowest level of the room, grading upward toward the back of the room. The small students sat in the front, the larger and older ones in the back.

There was no ventilation in the rooms; however, if windows could be opened, the teacher periodically did so to freshen the air within. There is some comment about the inadequacies of school buildings in the eighteenth century, but the real onslaught against them came in the middle of the nineteenth century, when laws were passed in several states ordering the attendance of all children. County superintendents, elected or appointed, visited the school operating in their districts and made recommendations for their improvement. Sometimes heeded, sometimes not, so that buildings continued to tumble down as they had been.

The Public School Law passed in Pennsylvania in 1834 required that children between the ages of six and fourteen be required to attend schools. Similar laws were passed in other states and schools came under scrutiny as they never had before. Reports of several state superintendents were published in *School Architecture Or The Contributions To The Improvement Of School Houses In United States*, by Henry Barnard, New York, 1849.

These reports make it evident that "all Hell broke loose" in the criticism of one-room schoolhouses. These comments are focused on the buildings which were built in the late eighteenth and early nineteenth centuries. One of the most damaging reports was made by the Secretary of the Board of Commissioners of Common Schools in 1838-1839 for the State of Connecticut.

I present with much hesitation the result of my examinations as to several hundred schoolhouses in different parts of the state. I will say generally, that the location of the schoolhouses instead of being retired, shaded, and attractive, in some cases are decidedly unhealthy, exposed freely to sun and storm, and nearly all, on one or more public streets where the passing objects, the noise and dust are a perpetual annoyance to teacher and scholar, ...that no playground is afforded for the scholar except the highway, ...that the size is too small for the average attendance of scholars, that not one in a hundred has any provision for a constant supply of that indispensable element of health and life, pure air, except that the rents and crevices which time and wanton mischief have made; that seats and desks are not, in a majority of cases, adapted to children of different sizes and ages, but on the other hand are calculated to induce physical deformity and ill-health, and in a few instances (I state this on the authority of physicians who were profession-

ally acquainted with the cases) have actually resulted in this...and that the mode of warming the rooms, sufficient regard is not had either to the comfort and health of the scholar, or to the economy.

He further pointed out that there was no wonder that children acquired a distaste for study and developed a reluctance to attend school after sitting on the uncomfortable benches; breathing and rebreathing the foul air around them, they tended to go to sleep and frequently needed to be aroused.

In some schools the students confronted the teacher (as they should), but in others they faced the wall or the center of the room. The larger students sat on backless benches facing the wall. To recite they had to turn around and lean their backs against the shelf which functioned as their desk. This procedure was particularly embarrassing to the female pupils.

Seventy-five districts had closed stoves for heating the room; in twenty-three there were stoves and fireplaces, and six had fireplaces alone. None of the buildings had any provision for ventilation and none a scraper to remove mud from the shoes before entering the building.

Looking at the outside of the school, the same man pointed out that there was no playground except the highway, and eighty-nine one-room schools stood entirely or partly on the highway. In another county, out of sixteen schools, most of them were on a highway and several were bounded by two roads. Neatness was not nurtured by a special place for wraps and lunches. He counted 176 pieces of broken glass, the holes being stuffed with hats, caps, and other applicable objects. Twenty-eight had never been whitewashed and none had blinds.

The commissioner was generally discouraged by the lack of maps, globes, and other school apparatus. Virtually no building had a second room for the recitation of classes nor a private place for the teacher to confer with parents. Only a few had sufficient interest in their children to inquire of the teacher about them.

There were no libraries, and only a few blackboards. Some rooms had many windows so that light glared onto the books while being read. Others had too few windows, sometimes ill-placed. Crevices in the floor helped to circulate cold air around the feet of the scholars, while elsewhere the door sill and other parts had rotted away. It was not uncommon to have the teacher and the students huddled around the stove in the center of the room. No schools had thermometers or clocks.

The Superintendent of Michigan made a lengthy report in 1847, with particular emphasis on the evils in arranging desks in one-room schoolhouses. Students on the outer perimeter of the building had the typical inconvenience of facing the wall when studying, but of turning around facing the teacher when reciting. Scholars ranged along three sides of the schoolroom, omitting the fourth where the teacher's desk was located. But, a more unfortunate problem was a long desk where ten students sat. This seating plan caused inconvenience when a student near the center wanted to get out. However, he often by-passed the others by crawling over his desk. Such an arrangement also prevented the teacher from giving individual help to the pupils sitting near the center.

A problem with the construction of desks arose when they had closed fronts reaching from the top of the desk to the floor. This arrangement prevented free circulation of fresh air, with the result that students often had cold feet and legs unless the room was kept unusually warm.

The Commissioner's secretary was particularly unhappy with the size and height of the seats and desks. He commented as follows:

I have visited many schools in which the majority of scholars reverse the ordinary practice of standing up and sitting down. They literally sit up and stand down, their heads being higher while sitting than standing.

He further commented about the facilities of the average schoolhouse:

Schoolhouses are not generally furnished with suitable conveniences for disposing of loose wearing apparel of the children, their dinners, etc. There are sometimes a few nails or shelves in a common entry through which scholars pass, upon which a portion of their clothes may be hung or laid. But in such cases the outside door is usually left open, the rain and snow beat in, and the scholars, in haste to get their own clothes, frequently pull down many more, which are trampled underfoot. Moreover, the dinners are frozen and not unfrequently devoured by dogs, and even by hogs that run in the street.

This official commented further about the stoves used in one-room schoolhouses. He stated that it was not uncommon to find stoves that were cracked, doors without hinges, and a latch and rusty stovepipe of various sizes. There were no woodsheds or other facility for the protection of fuel from snow and rain. This situation, in addition to the usual amount of green wood, caused the stoves to smoke, particularly in stormy weather. He said he heard trustees say that "they really didn't know the room was so smoky; we must get some new pipe; really our stoves are getting dangerous, etc." And some boys had relieved the embarrassment by saying, "It don' smoke near as bad today as it does sometimes."

Although he might have sounded ridiculous at the time, the Superintendent in Michigan said that every school should have the following articles:

1. *An evaporating dish for the stove.*
2. *A thermometer for checking the temperature.*
3. *A clock for regulating class activities.*
4. *A shovel and tongs.*
5. *An ash pail and ash house.*
6. *A wood house well supplied with wood.*
7. *A well to provide pure drinking water.*
8. *And last, though not least in this connection, two privies in the rear of the schoolhouse, separated by a high close fence, one for the boys and the other for girls, for want of these indispensable appendages the delicacy of children is frequently offended and morals corrupted.*

His final tirade was against the appearance of one-room schoolhouses.

In architectural appearance schoolhouses had more resembled barns, sheds for cattle, or mechanic shops than temples of science; windows are broken, benches mutilated, desks and cut wood are unprovided, obscene images and vulgar delineations meet the eye without and within. The plastering is smoked and patched, the roof is open to let in a flood of water in a storm sufficient to drown out the school, if the floor were not equally open.

It is interesting to note that the final report in the book by previously mentioned Dr. Barnard deals with a subject the most offensive of all. As a matter of fact, the writer, who attended a one-room school, remembers some of the activity mentioned in this report. However, the carving on desks was usually confined to students' initials or a heart with an arrow piercing it. It is not likely that such activity extended to the doors and windows, or a nearby rail fence.

Although lengthy, the following report is a sad commentary about what was easily seen in and around schoolhouses in the late eighteenth and early nineteenth centuries.

It is a humbling fact that in many of these houses there are highly indecent, profane and libidinous marks, images, and expressions, some of which are spread out in broad characters on the walls, where they meet the eyes of all who come within the house, or being on the outside, salute the traveler as he passes by, wounding the delicatena, annoying the sensibilities of the heart. While there is still a much greater number in small characters, upon the tables and chairs of the students, and even in some instances the instructors, constantly before the eyes of those who occupy them. How contaminating these must be, no one can be entirely insensible. And yet unalarmed, if not entirely unalarmed, how little is the mind of the community directed to the subject, and how little effort put forth to stay this fountain of corruption. We will mention, as evidence of the public apathy, one house which we suppose is this day, it certainly was a few months since, defiled by images and expressions of the kind referred to, spread out in open observation upon its walls, which are known to have been there for eight or ten years. In this building during all this time, the summer and winter schools have been kept; here the district held their business meetings; here frequently has been the singing school; here, too, religious meetings have often been held; here, too, the school committee, the fathers, mothers, and friends of the children have come to witness the progress of their children in knowledge and virtue, all of whom must have witnessed, and been ashamed of their defilement, and yet no effort has been put forth to remove them. Such things ought not to be; they can, to a considerable extent, be prevented. The community are therefore not altogether clear in the matter.

A two-story log schoolhouse located near Bernville, Berks County, Pennsylvania. The first floor is the "spring room" named for a spring of water available to the students.

 3

Nineteenth-Century Idealism

Because of the inadequacies in the construction of early school buildings, there was an enormous demand for plans to improve these edifices. This demand was met by some outstanding leaders in the field of education. A number of books were published about 1850 for school boards to follow in supplying the local need for buildings and apparatus. The following material is drawn from the publications, and there is no guarantee that all facets of recommendations were met; however, some of the practices trickled down to the early twentieth century, proving that "sooner or later" school buildings and desks were greatly improved.

Recommendations were based on a fine humanitarian feeling for the youth of the country, and an endless supply of building materials which lay at the footsteps of the builders. The results were crude by today's standards, but they were a pronounced improvement over earlier practices.

13

Front location of the schoolhouse on the grounds, with a fence and a gate surrounded by trees.

The first consideration in the construction of a one-room schoolhouse was the location and size of a site. This matter required much deliberate thought, for early sites were selected because they were unsuitable for any other purpose. One building had a stone at a corner to keep passing vehicles from scraping the edge of the building. If possible, the schoolhouse should look over a delightful landscape with a slight rise toward the north to partially protect the playground from harsh winds. Swamps and low spots were absolutely unthinkable.

Experts were unanimous in suggesting the school property should be rectangular in shape, with no irregular indentations. For economy in purchasing the site, the shorter dimension should be along the street or road. If lots were located in a village it was thought desirable to build on a corner lot to increase its accessibility from two streets, and thus reduce the need for students crossing them. School directors were warned that the safety of pupils should be a major concern, particularly the very young who attend the primary grades.

For normal use the lot should never be smaller than a half acre and rarely larger than one acre. If a whole acre was not always available in a solidly built-up village, a smaller lot could be used near the center of the town, or a larger one at a less convenient spot on the outskirts. In either case the site should be accessible to a large portion of the school population. A picket fence around the grounds would help to keep students off the street and discourage passers-by from trespassing on the grounds. A gate leading to a gravel footpath should be provided within the fence, as well as a larger one for use if vehicles had to enter the school grounds.

The next problem was to locate the building on the site selected. In most cases it was recommended that it be built on the front half of the lot so that an adequate play yard was available at the back. Space for play and exercise was stressed in all the recommendations. Care was also to be taken to keep the structure away from the road or street so students would not be distracted by activity there.

Considerable attention was given to the geographical orientation of the building. It was pointed out that light from the north was never blinding from bright sunshine, but comment was also made that it was lifeless and unattractive. Bright sunshine was acceptable if controlled by blinds or curtains.

Enough trees should be planted throughout the playground to provide shade in very hot weather and to assist students in learning the names of various species. An excerpt from *School Architecture*, by Henry Barnard, describes an ideal procedure for planting trees.

Tall trees should partially shade the grounds, not in stiff rows or heavy clumps, but scattered irregularly as if by the hand of nature.... The border of a natural wood may often be chosen for the site of the school; but if it is thinned out or trees are to be planted, and for a limited space, a selection is to be made, the kingly magnificent oaks, the

14

stately hickories, the spreading beech for its deep mass of shade, the maples for their rich abundant foliage, the majestic elm, the useful ash, the soft and graceful birches, and the towering sycamore, claim precedence. Next may come the picturesque locusts, with their hanging fragrant flowers; the tulip tree; the hemlock, best of evergreens; the celtis, or sweet gum; the nyssa, or tupelo; the walnut and the butternut: the native poplar; and the aspen.

The growing of flowers and bushes in the school yard is a far cry from conditions fifty years earlier. However, with constant demands for such landscaping, it is likely that some teachers complied with them. Their care, of course, fell upon the shoulders of the teachers unless they were able to get older pupils to help them. School finances were very tight, so no janitor or local handyman could be employed to look after the schoolhouse and the grounds. The motive for beautifying the school yard was to help students identify plants and to encourage their parents to grow flowers around their own homes. It might also be pointed out that since the school was a community center for meetings of all types, it could become an example of good housekeeping for the adults to see it.

Because of the inexperience of school directors in matters of building public structures, some very precise directions were given for them to follow. Before construction started, all the dirt and rubbish was to be dug out for excavating the cellar. The dirt thus obtained could be used for grading the school yard around the building on an incline of one inch to a foot.

Not all buildings had cellars, but those constructed were to be seven feet between the floor and the ceiling beams. The footers were to be "puddled and rammed" to a perfect bed, and those to the main walls and piers were to be entirely laid below the level of the cellar floor. The walls were to be laid up of sound building stone, using lime mortar. The specification of lime mortar was a very important procedure for earlier walls were often laid up with mud in which animal hair was mixed. After many driving rains the mud was often "washed out," and then had to be replaced to keep a sound wall. The wall above the ground level was to be neatly pointed, the inside surface to be well dashed with mortar. The chimney was to be built of hard-burned bricks, particularly above the roof line. One expert recommended that a cellar window be made under each of the upper windows; however, this was obviously an optional procedure.

The following specifications were for a frame building at a minimum cost.

The sills will be six by eight inches of white oak; all other timbers of white pine or hemlock; corner posts four by six (inches), plates, ties, and braces four by five, and studding three by four, flooring joists three by twelve inches, backed, with half inch crown, and two lines of lattice bridging well secured to the same; the ceiling joists two by ten inches; and the rafters to be the usual cut, and joists, studding and rafters to be placed sixteen inches between centers; the rafters to be well nailed at the heel, and the top to be secured by nailing upright boards on the face of the rafters and ceiling joists. The rafters are to be lathed and covered with the best pine shingles, butted and joined. The building to be carefully framed throughout, and draw bored and pinned, and braces dovetailed at one end. The weather boarding to be ploughed and overdropped.

Plans are provided in *Pennsylvania School Architecture*, Thomas H. Burrowes, Editor, Harrisburg, 1855, for a number of school buildings, each one varying in size and the materials of which they are constructed. Another plan for a frame building suggests the use of vertical boarding. The boarding was to be planed and beveled, and strips three inches wide nailed over the joints.

Considerable attention was given to the materials and construction of windows. The most important suggestion was to have the window sash hung with "the best axle pulleys, patent sash, cord and weights." Each window was to have a pair of shutters, sunken panels on one side, well hinged and secured when open. Small ventilating windows under the roof level were filled with slats for ventilation.

In most buildings, windows were placed in the two long sides of the rectangle. Planners were very emphatic in suggesting that none be located at the front of the room, so that no students had to face into a glaring light. Some windows might be placed in the rear wall, provided that they were screened out by the smaller rooms at the back end (library, apparatus, etc.). They were to be very tall and the bottom sash was to be filled with frosted glass if action or antics outside were likely to disturb the study habits of scholars. Also, the windows were to be equipped with blinds, and some fastidious teachers are known to have provided curtains also.

The interior walls were to be lathed (small wooden strips on which plaster was laid) and plastered with two coats of brown mortar and one of hard finish; the brown mortar was to be

Octagonal schoolhouse at Cowgill's Corner is one of the earliest one-room schools in Delaware. Built in 1836 in an eight-sided design, it was believed that this design would create more space and light. This was District No. 12 School in Kent County until 1930. Courtesy: The Division of Historical and Cultural Affairs, Delaware.

composed of fresh wood-burnt lime, and clean sharp sand, well aired. The lower sides of the walls were to be wainscoted (narrow vertical strips of wood) the height of the windowsills, and capped on a line with the same. Washboard was to be fitted along the floor of the main room as well as the clothes room and library. Pin rails were to be installed in each clothes room, and three dozen best wardrobe hooks secured on the rails.

Adequate doors were to be provided through the building, the exterior ones to be one and three-fourth inches thick having four panels and molded on the outside, hinged on four-inch butts, and secured with a good rim lock with several keys.

An opening eighteen inches in diameter was made in the ceiling for ventilation.

All the woodwork painted with three coats of pure white lead and the best linseed oil, finished in plain colors as the directors suggest. The sash was to be glazed with the best American glass, sprigged and back puttied. The size of the glass was to be twelve by sixteen inches with eighteen lights (panes) in each frame.

Although no firm estimate was made of the cost for such a building, the "round figure" suggested was $550.

These specifications were for a basic inexpensive building. Other suggestions dealt with matters such as masonry walls, hoods over the

entries, and a bell tower on the roof. The inclusion of a "ventiduct" was among other internal improvements, such a facility being of much importance in more sophisticated buildings. The highest cost of a one-room building was projected at $1,100.

Plans were also very specific for the internal arrangements of the buildings. Planners were almost unanimous in their demand for recitation rooms in addition to the main schoolroom and rooms for apparatus and a library. The library was to be used not only by the pupils, but also for the parents when they attended various town meetings in the school.

Search for the ideal schoolhouse seems never to have ended, as indicated by the fact that a rather large number were built in an octagonal shape. These appear on the eastern seaboard in many localities, and quite a few survive today. Various agencies have assumed the responsibility for keeping them in good repair so later generations can see how their elders were educated in these novel buildings.

Several examples are illustrated in the *Octagon Fad* by Carl Schmidt. Among them is one at Sutton's Corner, New York; one in Florence, Ohio; another in Penn's Grove, Pennsylvania; and one at Marcellus, New York. All are different from each other and from the one illustrated in *School Architecture.*

The advantages of the octagonal form are enumerated in *School Architecture* as follows:

1. The least quantity of wall is needed for such an inclosure.

2. The roof is constructed without tie beams, the lower end of the rafters being held by wall plates, the other by the frame of the lantern.

3. Light, ventilation, and a uniform temperature are secured from the lantern in the roof.

4. Light from the lantern is distributed evenly throughout the room, thus avoiding shadows.

5. Side windows can be used only for ventilation. (One of the plans has windows high in the wall so students could not see outside.)

6. There will be less broken glass with windows at a high level.

7. The source of heat is in the center of the room, and all areas will be equally heated.

8. The arrangement of seats is parallel with the sides of the building, which is a convenient arrangement.

9. The students can sit facing the wall, so they are not distracted by activity within the building.

10. The teacher can sit in the middle of one of the flat walls, and thus command the attention of all the students.

11. The lobby next to the front door can be made large for recitation purposes.

12. The stovepipe is unobtrusive as it rises directly above the stove and exits in the center of the lantern light.

13. The face of the wall opposite can have a door leading to a woodhouse, and beyond it are the privies.

14. The woodhouse is open on two sides to permit air passage to dry the wood.

15. Without the beams (tie) the ceiling can be left open up to the rafters, providing an excellent air space for the students.

Construction of an octagonal building was not greatly different from that of a rectangular one. No basement was mentioned, though a good footer of stone was to go as deep as the frost line. The super structure was framed and covered with 1-1/2-inch planks, tongued and grooved in order to avoid the expense of a fillet to cover the joint. A rustic effect could be obtained by log construction, but corner joining would be much more difficult than those for rectangular buildings. The only two octagonal schoolhouses known to the writer are of stone, which would be substantial and long lasting.

Particular attention had to be given to have the octagonal form create a strong loop to withstand the outward thrust of the rafters. Such strength was effected by having the plates form overlapping ties.

A ventilating device could be constructed in the center of the roof lantern. This was the most advantageous place for foul air to exit, without causing drafts upon the students as they sat at their desks.

Probably the most famous octagonal schoolhouse in the country is one known as the Diamond Rock School, located in the north valley of Chester County, Pennsylvania, two and one-half miles from Paoli. The building of this school is a perfect example of the construction of a neighborhood school. It is reported that in 1818 a native of the area recognized the need for a school, and a meeting was called to consider the matter. A Mr. Beaver donated a tract of land at a point between two roads to be used for 999 years. A parchment deed survives as a testimony of this act.

The original agreement under which the land was granted and the building erected follows:

Whereas, George Beaver, Jr., of Tredyffrin Township, Chester County, and State of Pennsylvania, has agreed and doth hereby agree to lees Twenty perches of Land, to such of the neighbors as may Subscribe their names hereunto for the purpose of Erecting a School-house for the use of the said subscribers, for and during the term of Nine-hundred and ninety-nine years.

We, the subscribers, do therefore promise to pay the respective sums opposite our names for the purpose above mentioned, in the following manner- One halfe of Subscription money to be paid by each of us as soon as the Building is begun- The other halfe, as soon as it is finished- the Money to be paid to such Subscribers as maybe agreed upon by a Majority.

This act was drawn up on January 12, 1818, when the subscription list on the next page was formed, a reprint of which is posted on the wall of the restored building.

Jacob Beidler	30 dolls.	John Shriver	5
Ezekial Potts	5	John Hawk	3
Wm. Potts	10	John Rickenbaugh	3
James Sloan	20	William Banks	2.50
Jacob Longacre	9	Adam Harner	2.50
Jno. Beaver	10	Jacob Rickabaugh	10
Israel Davis	8	Jonathan Brooks	2.50
David Beaver	5	John Steward	5
Ann McMinn	1	Erasmus Laver	.50
Joseph Watson	5	Jacob Rennard	2
Johan Campbell	3	David Ruth	5
John Dempsey	5	Adam Rickabaugh	12
Hanery Place	3	John Kugler Sr.	5
Jacob Steward	4	Samuel Jones	5
Jesse More	5	Charles Rowland	3

Two of the subscribers to this agreement wrote their names in German script and they cannot be identified. The founders of the school were settlers of German and Welsh descent. It is reported that the final cost of the school was $260.93.

The curriculum of the school contained the usual subjects of reading, writing, arithmetic, grammar, spelling, geography, history, and, at times, surveying was included. Its most unusual function, however, was during the 1830s when a "Young Men's Debating Society" was maintained for several seasons. For this activity the room was lighted with tallow candles, each member being taxed a levy of .12 1/2 to pay for fuel and light. Its roll contained the names of nearly all the middle-aged men in the vicinity. Two judges were appointed, and from eight to ten men assigned to each side. Subjects were debated such as "Resolved, that it would be a sound policy to abolish capital punishment," and "Is the mind of mankind naturally more inclined to a civilized or savage life?"

For fifty years the building was used, usually being filled with sixty to sixty-five pupils. All the students sat on benches without backs, and in the center were two short rows of desks on which small children sat. In the center was a ten-plate stove in which large chunks of wood were burned. The farmers donated large sizes of wood, which the larger boys sawed and chopped to a useable size. In 1864 the building was overcrowded and the student body was divided between two new schools, the "Walker" and the "Salem."

Time and the elements had their way with the beloved structure; however, a new destiny for it came upon the scene in the twentieth century. Led by Miss Emma Wersler, a permanent organization assumed the task of restoring the school and forming an organization known as the "Diamond Rock Old Scholars Association." A feature of this organization's purpose was that each year there should be a reunion held at the school. This provision has been faithfully followed, and the excellent condition of the building and grounds is a tribute to the effectiveness of the organization. Similar organizations have been formed at other one-room schools, all of which wish to perpetuate the ideals and function of these venerated buildings.

It is a strange coincidence that two octagonal schoolhouses survive in Chester County, Pennsylvania, and there is considerable data about them. The octagonal building close to the Birmingham Meetinghouse built in 1818 was not the first one built in the area. There was one built in 1756. It is described in early accounts as a plain square building of logs, and stood on the side of the road toward Strode's mill, on the site of the hay and wagon house on the Garrett property. It was a small building with a low ceiling so the students could hang their dinner baskets on the joists. Such a display would obviously have been a very picturesque sight.

It was taught for many years by John Forsythe who came from Ireland as a young man, and became a member of Birmingham Friend's meeting. His salary was made up by the neighbors who agreed to furnish him one or more students annually at the rate of eight dollars per student. Nearly fifty years later the price of teaching rose to ten and twelve dollars per year. In Forsythe's time, about twenty students attended school, nearly all boys. It was thought not worthwhile to educate girls, except in household matters.

At a meeting of school subscribers on May 15, 1819, Edward Darlington was chosen chairman and Isaac Sharpless, secretary. It was found that it would cost $259 to repair the old school building and $534 to build a new one. It was decided to build a new structure, and a list of subscribers is in the archives of the Chester County Historical Society in West Chester, Pennsylvania. A total of $732 was subscribed. There is a lease of 999 years on the ground with an annual rent of one ear of Indian corn to be paid on demand.

An octagonal structure of stone was built, covered with plaster as it is today. Benches were made by cutting the logs in half, with the flat side turned up. Desks were correspondingly rough. Later, improved desks and chairs replaced the earlier furniture, and a curtain was hung from the ceiling to break reverberations of sound in the building.

Older boys attended the school in the winter when the enrollment reached as high as sixty. Younger children attended school in the spring and summer. Years after its construction, men were

Octagonal schoolhouse located on the grounds of the Birmingham Meeting-house in Chester County, Pennsylvania. Its location on the church grounds suggest a close collaboration with the church authorities.

engaged to teach in the winter, and when summer sessions were held, they were taught by women.

The school was known as Harmony Hall, and it served the community until 1859 when a shift in the population caused it to close. It was unused until 1874 when it was fitted out for persons attending funerals in the nearby burying ground. In 1895, as the population returned to the Birmingham region, it was again used as a school. However, by 1905 another population shift due to industrialization saw the end of its use as a school.

The source of heat was a very live subject, for stoves were just coming into use when most of these plans were formulated. Only two in *School Architecture* call for the use of fireplaces, which were noted for roasting students nearby while others shivered on the outer edges. Considerable attention was given to the Franklin fireplace, which was designed to circulate hot air in the room. As a matter of fact, plans were included to construct a similar device of bricks.

One of the floor plans with a fireplace was designed to accommodate forty-eight pupils. The following is an explanation of the various parts of that schoolroom.

Heating a schoolroom with a stove was some improvement over the use of an open fireplace. However, there continued to be hot and cold spots in various parts of the rooms. In several of the floor plans the

stove was set up at the front of the room, probably a residual of the earlier location of the fireplace. With the stove at the front, the room eventually became warm; however, the heat was not distributed evenly as if it were in the center of the room. An unnamed committee, probably in

SCHOOL FOR FORTY-EIGHT PUPILS.

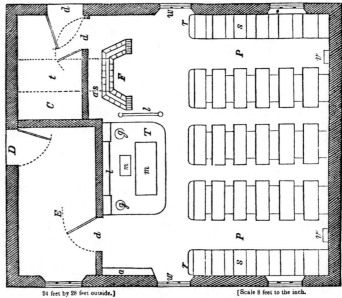

24 feet by 28 feet outside.] [Scale 8 feet to the inch.

D. Entrance door. E. Entry. F. Fireplace. C. Wood closet, or recitation room T. Teacher's platform. a. Apparatus shelves. t. Air tube beneath the floor. d. Doors g. Globes. l. Library shelves. m. Master's table and seat. p. Passages. r. Recitation seats. s. Scholars' desks and seats. v. Ventilator. w. Windows. b. Movable blackboard. a. s. Air space behind the fireplace.

Credit: *School Architecture or Contributions to the Improvement of Schoolhouses in the United States.*

the Boston area, was commissioned to investigate the stoves or furnaces available for school use. In *School Architecture*, a report appeared of the virtues of one invented by a Mr. Chilson. A partial description follows:

It is simple in its construction, easily managed, will consume fuel perfectly, and with a moderate fire. It is fitted for wood or coal. The fireplace is broad and shallow, and is lined with soapstone or fire brick, which not only makes it perfectly safe and durable, but modifies very materially the usual effect of the fire upon the iron pot.

The principal radiating surfaces are wrought iron, of a suitable thickness for service, while at the same time heat the smallest fire is communicated to the air chamber.

On this stove, air was brought from the outside through a tube under the floor, and then passed through a metal inclosure or jacket some distance from the furnace itself.

Air never entered the inner portion of the stove, with the result there was no "burnt air" in the schoolroom, such air being considered unhealthy. The committee claimed the outer jacket never became hot enough to injure a person, but a constant flow of hot air within certainly must have made it uncomfortable to touch. The writer's one-room schoolhouse was heated by a pot-bellied stove of cast iron which became so hot that the metal turned a low red. A sheet-metal screen inclosed the stove, except where refueling and removing the ashes was done. The screen became just hot enough to dry outer garments hung on it, for which purpose it had to be kept perfectly clean.

One of the mandates in a teacher's contract was that the room had to be heated to a comfortable temperature by the students' arrival in the morning. This meant that the teacher had to be in the room an hour before classes were called; but female teachers often employed a mature boy to get the fire started in the morning. If wood was burned, the fire had to be started from "scratch;" if coal, the dead ashes had to be shaken out of the bottom of the fire and draft turned on. In either case, the disposal of ashes was difficult. Of course, both a wood and a coal fire dried out the air, a condition which was resolved by placing a pan of water on the top of the stove to dampen the air for the comfort of the pupils.

The best mode for heating the one-room school was to place a furnace in the cellar and have pipes conduct heat to various parts of the room. The virtues of such a plan are mentioned appropriately in *School Architecture*.

No portion of the room, movements of the scholars, or the supervision of the teacher are unencumbered or interrupted by the stove or the pipe. The fire in such places can be maintained without noise and without throwing smoke or dust into the room.

The offensive odors and impurities of burnt air, or rather particles of vegetable or animal matter floating in the air, are not experienced. The heat can be conducted into the room at different points, and is thus diffused so as to secure a uniform heat in every part of it.

If a teacher were sensitive to the fluctuations of heat in different parts of the room, the condition could be monitored with a thermometer. Additional listing of supplies for every instructor included a coal bucket, clock, brooms and mops, and cloths to wash the blackboards when they could no longer be satisfactorily cleaned with erasers.

In all discussions of the one-room schoolhouse, more space is devoted to the subject of ventilation than to any other. A lengthy exposition of lung action in absorbing oxygen from the fresh air focuses attention on the results of breathing and re-breathing impure air. It points out that:

If this process is long continued, even though the air is slightly deteriorated, the effects will be evident in the languid and feeble actions of the muscles, the sunken eye, the squalid hue of the skin, unnatural irritability of the nervous system, a disinclination to all mental and bodily action, and a tendency to stupor, headache, and fainting.

The sensitivity of the officials to this problem of poor ventilation is detailed in the ill effects of breathing impure air. It is recounted that in 1756 about 146 prisoners were incarcerated in the so-called "Black Hole of Calcutta." With only two small windows to permit the entry of fresh air, all the prisoners struggled to get near the windows. The cries for fresh air and water were constant, and while a few reached the window, others fell and were trod upon in the violent action. When the doors were opened eleven hours later, 123 prisoners had died of suffocation and the remainder lay on the floor with a

Farm animals grazing next to the Miller one-room schoolhouse at Greenfield Village. This is a typical schoolhouse of the late nineteenth century. Courtesy: Henry Ford Museum and Greenfield Village.

putrid fever. A Dr. Combe comments about the situation in his *Principles Of Physiology:*

> *This terrible example ought not to be lost upon us, and if results so appalling arise from the extreme corruption of the air, results less obvious and sudden, but no less certain, may be expected from every lesser degree of impurity.*

The conclusion to be drawn from that incident is that in the schoolroom the same poisoning process goes on day after day; and considering the large number of schoolrooms in America, the results were predicted to be catastrophic. But the condition was not only detrimental to the students, but also to the teachers. It is asserted that after teachers have worked for several years in this confined atmosphere, they either become irritated and exhausted from their daily tasks, or simply quit their jobs. As a

matter of fact, consumption and other dire effects were also predicted.

Curiously, the open fireplace, which was so wasteful of heat, did effect a reasonable amount of ventilation in the room in which it was located. The column of hot air going up the chimney swept with it the mass of air nearest the floor. Although there were no ducts for introducing fresh air into the room, much of the foul air was removed.

After stoves were introduced and the tightness of the building improved, the common procedure for ventilation was to open the doors and windows. Teachers were warned that this was a frightful procedure when the students were still inside, for the blast of cold air struck their backs and chilled them. Such a ventilating, however, could be practiced at recess when the students were active out of doors when the weather was reasonably mild.

With some types of stoves a tube was extended to the outer wall of the building, permitting the entry of fresh air through the floor just under the stove, where it was circulated by the convection of hot air in a confined area. The common recommendation was to provide an opening or two at the top of the building which could be regulated from the floor level with a rod or a string.

In the middle of the nineteenth century there was not only a renaissance in the building of school structures, but there were innovations within them. The fireplace was replaced by a stove, new and improved seats and desks were used, and provisions were made to locate a library within the four walls of the main building. This accommodation took the form of shelves, preferably in back of the teacher's desk, or a separate room. A plan was suggested by the famous Horace Mann that one end of the room be subdivided into three smaller areas. On the outer two sides were separate entries for the girls and boys. Between these two small rooms a library was located to accommodate a substantial number of books. Henry Barnard reports in *School Architecture* that:

The schoolhouse is the appropriate depository of the district library, and a library of well selected books, open to the teacher, children, and adults generally of the district, for reference and reading, gives completeness to the permanent means of the school and self-education, which can be embraced in the arrangement of a schoolhouse.

He goes on to tell that the books might serve the teacher in advancing her knowledge of any particular subject which she was teaching. And there might well be books of a professional nature to compensate for her poor preparation for her vocation.

The library should contain books adapted to the needs of the youngest students which will help in giving them a high standard in manners, morals, and intellectual attainments. There should also be some for housewives, farmers, mechanics, and tradesmen. The books should shed light on the dignity of their work, and help them to understand world-wide activities with which they will never have any personal contact. The rich can always secure personal books for their information, but a school library must be accessible to the poor who cannot afford books. Barnard concludes by saying that:

The establishment of a library in every schoolhouse will bring the mighty instrument of good books to act more directly and more broadly on the entire population of the state, than it has ever yet done, for it will open the fountains of knowledge without money, and without price, to the humble and the elevated, the poor and the rich.

It is likely that all states did not "jump into the act immediately." However, it is known that in 1838 the legislature of New York State passed an act providing funds for a library in each school district. The idea of a free school library had much public appeal, and in the years following the act, Governor Seward reported that of the 11,000 schools in the state, only a very few had not taken some action in establishing libraries.

In a report written by David L. Salay in 1975, he points out:

One reason for the enthusiasm was the scarcity of books in America. While many families had a small library, and a few individuals (usually doctors and lawyers) had a collection of 500 or more volumes, the private libraries of central New York's farmers and mechanics was small. In addition to a Bible or almanac, they numbered few volumes. With few outside attractions, a public library, to illuminate the mind and transport the imagination to other times and distant places, was most appealing. Few districts failed to take advantage of the opportunity (to establish a library).

Fifty thousand dollars were allocated for the establishment of district libraries by the legislature of New York, which was a sizable amount out of a total of $160,000 school budget. Money was continued on a yearly basis with each school district being responsible to allocate an equal amount. Because books cost an average of twenty cents each, it is obvious that over a period of years a sizable library could be established. By 1849 the library of Hartwick district contained 177 volumes.

It is interesting to note that in New York State the teacher did not buy the books, nor did she administer the library. The school trustees, or some people appointed by them, selected the books, and a responsible adult charged them "in and out." The content of the books was a matter of quality rather than having a large number of inadequate books.

In 1838 a Boston book company published lists from which selections could be made, and the following year Harper Brothers suggested books to be taken from their list of 250 volumes. Books about geography, philosophy, science, and kindred subjects were bought. Among them could have been:

A System of Natural Philosophy, by J. L. Comstock, New York, 1845.

The Infantry Exercise of the United States Army, Abridged for the Use of the Militia of the United States, Montpelier, Vermont, 1820.

Winter Evening Tales, Collected Among the Cottagers in the South of Scotland, by James Hogg, Philadelphia, 1836.

Literary and Scientific Class Book, by Levi W. Leonard, Boston, 1826.

A History of Inventions, Discoveries, and Origins, by John Beckman, London, 1846.

The American Politician, by M. Sears, Boston, 1842.

There were decided preferences in the selection of books taken out of school libraries in New York. Historical and biographical were first. Philosophy and religion were second. Travel and Geography were third; and science and mechanics were also liked. Although encyclopedias were probably not widely selected, the *Encyclopedia; or a Dictionary of Arts, Sciences, and Miscellaneous Literature*, with 542 copper plates printed in Philadelphia in the 1790s, was available, and later (1854) an issue of the *Americana Encyclopedia* was off the press.

From Henry Barnard's book and the report about libraries in New York State, one might get the idea that a library was a very common appendage to a one-room schoolhouse; however, in my limited experience in Pennsylvania, they were very uncommon in that state.

Another matter of much concern to school authorities was the erection of satisfactory privies on the rear of the school lot. Editor Burrowes tells in *Pennsylvania School Architecture*, that:

Injury to the bodily health of the young from unwholesome effluvia is the smallest portion of this evil. The indecency of the practice (poor privies) cannot be long continued without generating habits, whose very existence is proof of the absence of that sense of delicacy and of those finer feelings, which are indispensable to a high and correct moral character. When the sense of shame for doing that which is indecent is eradicated, one, and by no means the weakest, of the barriers against committing that which is honest, has also been removed.

The best place for the construction of privies was the extreme rear of the school grounds, putting the entrance doors toward the back fence providing privacy and the costs of screens. Two privies were always recommended. The buildings were to be erected over a well built round or oval cavity so the walls do not fall inward. The outward appearance of the buildings was to be as neat and ornamental as that of the main schoolhouse. They were to be of the same material, substantially finished and well painted. Some esthetes would train rose or ivy vines to add still more to its beauty, and by all evidence of good care, discourage vandals from marring its surface or distorting its form.

If privies were built of wood, inside surfaces did not need to be planed except for the boards of the seat. If of stone or brick, the inside walls were to be finished with a rough coat of plaster. In all cases, the walls were to be lime-washed with a dark color to discourage writing and drawing pictures.

Buildings for the two sexes were not to have a common wall. The central wall was to be hollow and lead to a louvered window near the top of the building, through which odors could easily escape. Hinged covers could be attached to the seats, with provision for them to close before the occupant leaves the building. Privies were to be locked after school hours, although the installation of locks was a waste of time for vandals were sure to break them.

In retrospect, it is evident that in the middle of the nineteenth century a great deal of attention was given to one-room school buildings. And, it must be stated that all the problems were not solved at that time. As a matter of fact, they never were.

The Boonetown one-room schoolhouse in Salt Township, Holmes County, Ohio, was purchased by the Amish when the public schools consolidated. The addition at the front of the building is a coal shed. To the rear are the outdoor toilets. Courtesy: Robert Mohr.

 **4**

Amish One-Room Schoolhouses

One would expect that with all the modern trends in education, the one-room schoolhouse would have disappeared; however, that is not the case, for in some areas they are not only surviving but they are increasing in number. These situations are occurring in Lancaster County, Pennsylvania, and Holmes County, Ohio. Some of the residents of these communities, and a few smaller regions in America, are not only separated from their neighbors in the matter of education, but also in most aspects of their daily life. Theirs is a socio-religious life, compared to

what they regard as the worldly life of others. To a large extent, their background accounts for their unique views.

In the seventeenth and early eighteenth centuries, this band of people lived in Switzerland and the upper Rhine Valley of Germany. "Pushed from pillar to post" by the secular authorities, these people were constantly harassed because of their resistance to war and their frugal religious life. These matters caused them to be separated from the large mass of population. Before coming to Pennsylvania, William Penn visited them in their homeland and advised them of the rich agricultural conditions in the New World.

The first immigrants from the region came to Lancaster County in the early part of the eighteenth century. Although they suffered untold hardships in their voyage to America, they wrote glowing letters about the attractions of their new homes.

These Germanic-based immigrants created a sub-culture that identified them as being different, particularly in their religious practices and their manner of farming. Some comment might be made about some of these views.

All decisions of their daily life are based on the contents of the Bible. The Amish consider themselves peculiar because the Bible says that God's children are peculiar and not conforming to the outside world. Their reference is Titus 2:11-14 and Romans 12:2. One obvious evidence in their difference is in their appearance. Amish men have long hair, banged across the front (not so strange today), and a straight cut across the back at their neck, called by many people a "crock" haircut. Unmarried men must shave, but married men have a beard, though they may not have a mustache. The mustache was part of the Prussian military image, and they wanted no part of that.

Their clothing is made in the home, the children wearing small models of that worn by adults. The men and boys wear broadfall trousers, made of unpatterned black, brown, or gray fabric, and broad-brimmed hats of felt or straw. The dress coats have no lapels, and openings in their clothing are secured by hooks and eyes. The Prussian use of bright buttons prohibited their use in America.

One of their major difference with orthodox religions (mainly Lutheran and Reformed) is their unacceptance of infant baptism. Amish feel that baptism should occur only after the child is old enough to make his or her own decision about the matter; however, as far as the Amish are concerned, they have only on choice, and that is to join the Amish sect.

A rule of their religion bars women from wearing any form of ornamentation. And, strange as it seems, the outer garments of the women are made of brightly colored fabrics such as blue and purple. They always wear a prayer covering on their head, and when they go away from their homes, they wear a simple bonnet, with a black shawl hung over their shoulders and closed in front.

The life of all communicants is controlled by the church. As a matter of fact, Amish have no church buildings, but in a well-regulated pattern, services are held in the homes of the members. There is no paid clergy, the leaders being chosen by a select group, pulling straws from the Bible. Farming is a requirement to stay in

Amish carpenters replacing a roof on a one-room school in Lancaster County, Pennsylvania.
Courtesy: Lancaster Newspapers.

good standing; however, blacksmithing, carriage building, and harness making are acceptable. Certain old and experienced men periodically meet and make decisions about the members' daily lives.

Perhaps the most notable regulation of the sect is that marriage must be kept within the group, and if a marriage occurs outside the group, the person has the chance to become a member or be "shunned." Shunning means that the person involved is prohibited from attending church services, and they are isolated in their family life. They cannot eat at the table with other members of their family; however, ironically, they are permitted to help with the farm work. In recent years a Mennonite man who was shunned by his family took the matter into a local court. This was a very unorthodox procedure, and it certainly has not resolved the problem. Generally speaking, the plain sects do not use the secular court to resolve their differences. They are settled by the elders of the church.

Within the house there cannot be any telephones, radios, or television sets. There cannot be electrical appliances of any type; however, a family refrigerator operated by gas is acceptable. Some of the farmers have large herds of cows, and their milk must be kept sanitary and cool, which requires a large refrigerator. Near the house is often a waterwheel or wind wheel, which pumps water from a spring and forces it to the house and an iron trough at the edge of the barnyard.

Members may not own automobiles; however, they may ride in one without forfeiting their entry into Heaven. Most farm equipment is powered by horses and mules, but a gasoline engine is allowed to turn threshing machines. A sizable number of the sect are carpenters who have a circular saw powered by a gasoline motor. The writer saw one saw powered by a motor designed to use on a lawn mower.

The Amish do not have insurance of any kind. If a barn is destroyed by fire, some skilled men lay out the joinery for a new barn, and on an appointed day male members gather at the site of the new barn and "raise" it. That means that the framework is erected at no cost to the owner of the barn. While work on the barn proceeds, the females of the sect prepare large amounts of food for the noonday meal and catch up on the local gossip. If a one-room schoolhouse is destroyed, the same action is pursued. In 1979 a schoolhouse burned in Lancaster County, and in two weeks a new building was provided, while classes met in a large home of a member. Amish carpenters are famous in Lancaster County for their ability to erect simple structures, mainly buildings used on a farm.

Not only do they replace schools, but they also build new ones. They are very sensitive to the cost of these buildings and carefully note that a building which cost $6,000 four years ago now costs $9,000. Building new schools is done in the summer by each member donating a day of work in each week until the building is finished. The only cost of construction is for the materials used. They have no plumbing or electricity. There are two privies in the yard, and lighting is provided by kerosene lamps placed along the walls of the schoolroom.

It seems rather obvious that the Amish would have specific and unusual means of educating their youths. Education is very significant to them, for they are aware that as a child grows, so it will live in its adult years. As long as there were one-room elementary schools in the countryside, the Amish seemed satisfied; however, when large consolidated schools came into use, they protested that their children should not attend them. The Amish insisted that education should stop at the age of fourteen and the eighth grade. The problem in their case came about because there was a state mandate that children attend school until the age of sixteen. This dilemma was solved for awhile by having Amish youths repeat grade eight until they were sixteen years old. This was obviously not a good procedure, and the Amish sometimes withheld their children from attending school after they were fourteen years old. This procedure resulted in fines and jail sentences, which also did not resolve the problem.

One of the early actions in Pennsylvania was the case of Levi and Samuel Beiler who refused to send two of their children to school in the 1930s. They were fined, and in their appeal of the fine they said that...

...they want to stop sending their two fourteen-year-old children to school because their continued attendance in school conflicted with the beliefs of the Amish church.

The two fathers contended that their children should be working on the farm instead of sending them to the Salisbury Township grade school.

The trial opened in a colorful court room. About 100 persons were present, including friends and neighbors of the two brothers. Small boys and girls were also in the audience. The two brothers were bearded and attired in Amish dress. They sat stolidly at the counsel table with solemn expressions on their faces.

The outcome of this appeal is not known; however, it probably was against the Amish for on February 8, 1938, they accrued their case to Governor Earle of Pennsylvania. Two strangely dressed men appeared at the governor's mansion in Harrisburg. Before being escorted to the drawing room, they left their broad-brimmed hats on a table in the hall.

The Governor joined them with a number of photographers, but they refused to be photographed. Thereafter, they were invited into the dining room where a table was set for a meal. In a style not common to the visitors, the elegant table setting consisted of large dinner plates richly decorated in blue and gold, the colors of Pennsylvania; a soup spoon, knife, fork, small butter plate with the state seal, and a water goblet completed the individual service.

The chair at the head of the table was occupied by the Governor, and at the other end sat a member of the visiting party. These visitors were in strange surroundings, compared to their modest life which they lived on their farms. Others in the party included Dr. Ackley from the State Department of Education; their counsel, Mr. Doyle; and the Deputy Attorney General, Mr. Thompson.

While the meal progressed the Governor commented that he was in favor of separate schools for the Amish because they warranted special consideration due to their long and fruitful residence in the Commonwealth. He also mentioned that Pennsylvania was famous for its tolerance and respect for the rights of its citizens.

Governor Earle continued by saying:

And for more than 150 years the state has guarded the liberties and rights of its citizens, and I propose to do all in my power to see that those liberties are still observed.

Thereupon, the butler entered with mushroom soup and the meal began. The main course of the meal was chicken with string beans and barley rice; chocolate cake was the dessert, and finger bowls were used.

After the meal the press was invited in and Governor Earle gave them a statement indicating that he was in favor of their request. He then left for an appointment at the capitol.

There was considerable wrangling in Pennsylvania about the matter of Amish youths attending school after they were fourteen years of age, but the main protest was to keep them from attending a high school in some distant place where the ideals of Amish society would be diluted and impaired. Finally, in 1956 an agreement was reached by the Amish community and the State Department of Education that the Amish could operate their own elementary one-room schools. The children could fulfill a school commitment until age sixteen by their daily work on the farm, of which they had to keep a diary and report to school three hours a week, preferably on Saturday morning, when they would be taught English, mathematics, social studies, and health.

Matters were to be resolved in other states and in 1972 a legal case before the State of Wisconsin and Amish families reached the Supreme Court of the United States.

The State argued that the government had the responsibility of educating the youth of the nation, and an Amish youth's lack of education would deter him from reaching his highest potential. The Amish fathers, Jonas Yoder, Adin Yutzy, and Wallace Miller, contended that the high school was too worldly and would teach the child values contrary to Amish beliefs. William Ball, the attorney for the Amish, said that a compulsory high school education could destroy the Amish community in America.

This was the first time the Supreme Court agreed to hear a case involving the Amish, and the first time such a case was based on the first amendment denying religious freedom. The case attracted widespread attention on the national press from educators and civil rights groups because it drew attention to the larger question: Should school attendance be compulsory in a free nation? Does the government have the right to force children to attend school?

The court's decision was in favor of the Amish. Justice Douglas wrote, in his opinion, that "the states should not prosecute Amish parents for keeping their children out of the state public school." Justice Byron White wrote, "I cannot say that the state's interest in requiring two more years of compulsory education in the ninth and tenth grades outweighs the importance of the concededly sincere Amish religious practice to the survival of the sect." Justices Stewart and Brennan concurred with White's statement. Blackman and Marshall also voted in favor of the Amish.

Chief Justice Warren Burger wrote:

Amish society emphasizes informal learning through doing, a life of goodness rather than a life of intellect; wisdom rather than technical knowledge; community welfare rather than competition; and separation rather than integration with contemporary society.

The evidence led the court to the inescapable conclusion that:

Secondary schools exposing Amish children to worldly influence...contravenes their basic religious tenets and practices of the Amish faith, both to parent and the child.

Kinsinger, the head of Amish schools in Lancaster County, said that discipline was one of their major concerns as he ticked off a list of values such as respect, sincerity, honesty, thrift, and cleanliness. He said, "If you have those, education will follow along with them."

Thus, it is evident that after long battles with the government agencies, the Amish had a mandate to establish and govern their own one-room elementary schools. They paid their local taxes and, in addition, underwrote all the cost of their parochial schools. Church officials supervised the schools in their district without pay. The only person paid in the organization was the teacher. In 1974 there were twenty-four schools in Pennsylvania, seventeen in Lancaster County.

The teachers are largely women whose major qualification is to have a high school diploma and an interest in working with children. After three years of service, new teachers are given a diploma which qualifies them to teach subjects in English and German in grades one to eight.

The basic curriculum consists of daily devotions, singing, arithmetic, spelling, geography, health, penmanship, English, and German. Classes run from 8:00 a.m. to 3:00 p.m. from Labor Day to Memorial Day, with two vacation days—Christmas and Good Friday. Today there is some use of duplicator machines, workbooks, and printed texts. Worldly gadgets are generally shunned in the classrooms. Student bodies range in size from twelve to fifty, with the average being twenty to thirty.

Before finishing the subject of Amish one-room schools, some attention should be given to one of their most popular diversions, the celebration of Valentine's Day. This idea is so unique that teachers from many parts of the nation correspond with Mrs. Beiler, a teacher in one of the schools in Lancaster County. Following is a report in the *Lancaster Sunday News*, February 13, 1955:

What makes the valentine unique is that the Amish children hold to the reverent old German custom of always starting a letter with a short biblical verse, reference, or greeting. Something like, "Greetings to you in the name of the Lord Jesus, and may He always be with you."

In the same spirit, Amish children write a short Bible greeting on their valentines just before their signature. As they are very artistic in Pennsylvania Dutch motifs of heart and flower designs, they have attracted the attention of art teachers in many States of the Union.

Unfortunately, some of the students are buying commercial cards for interchange between them. However, they still make some, especially for the teacher and their parents. Around their deft Pennsylvania designs they use a punch to imitate a lace edge, or heavy embroidery resembling the old-fashioned type that Grandma used to send. Of course, the teacher brings in some old ones to give the children ideas about how to make their own.

Another medium used by the students in the Beiler school is feed bags, in which the parents get feed or flour from the mill. Some packers hire designers to decorate their feed bags, and an estimated half billion bags are used in the country in a year. Pillow slips and other household items are made from the bags in school, even a few dresses.

The pupils realize in their sphere of living that their traditional folkways have become a pattern, and distant folks have beaten a path to their door. Among them is Margaret Divine, dean of Mills College in New York. She makes an annual trip to the Beiler school. Some write regularly, as does Margaret Dow from Boston.

This year's special valentines, which the youngsters have been making at school, will go mostly to their parents. One signed by the four small sons of one couple has this verse:

God's brilliant sunshine
From Heaven above
Our valentine yellow
Brings you our love.

5

The Teacher

The research about the one-room schoolhouse has led the writer into many channels. At this point the most important one is concerned with the teacher. There are really three facets to the study; namely, the schoolhouse, the books, and the teacher. Although each facet had some bearing on the education of our youth, the most important one was teaching. There may be poor buildings, and the supply of books may be meager, but these two deficiencies could be well compensated by the presence of a good teacher.

Before describing the role of the teacher, one should mention that the one-room schoolhouse was a very common institution in early New England, but less so in other parts of the country. The reason for its successful operation in the northeast lay in the fact that people lived close together in towns or parishes for greater protection from the Indians. Even so, Pilgrims found it expedient to carry guns on their way to church.

In those days people were very critical of the master, who had to possess a number of nonpedagogical qualifications. In addition to answering a multitude of questions about his religious faith, he had to be a good conversationalist, and certified by the town minister, plus the minister in an adjoining town. It is recorded that:

Selection by selectmen, election by the inhabitants in open town meetings, and approbation by the minister was the legal and narrow road to teaching.

Probably the most important facet of the teacher's work was in one way or another related to the minister and/or the church. More details will follow later. When Harvard was established in 1636, its major function was to prepare ministers and teachers, although there were no professional courses for either profession. The lowly position of the schoolmaster is revealed in the common practice of denoting the poorest preacher from the pulpit to the classroom, and promoting the best teachers to the ministry.

It is important to note that members of other professions were often associated with teaching. The first schoolmaster of Braintree was a physician, and it was understood that if a patient's case was urgent, he could close school and attend to his other duties. The doubling of a physician as a teacher more or less implied that he did not have steady work in how own profession, so he could fill in as a teacher. It is also possible that having another occupation would permit a teacher to accept a lower salary; for the mandates often given to selectmen was to hire the pedagogue "at the cheapest salary possible."

A unique combination of occupations is reported when a man was hired to teach in Grafton:

Reverend Aaron Hutch, who was an ordained pastor of the church here in 1750, not only united in himself the clergy and farmer, after the custom of the time, but also combined the clerical and agricultural with the pursuit of the office of teacher.

It was not uncommon to engage a teacher for a trial period of varying lengths. In 1671 a teacher was contracted in Stamford, Connecticut, with the understanding that his employment was not permanent. A few years later, it is recorded that the "town is not minded to hire Mr. Rider anymore." Apparently he was a native, whom the town regarded more as a liability than an asset. The committee consequently was advised not to hire an inhabitant of the town.

In 1722 a complaint was lodged against a teacher whose scholars were examined by a selectman and found to be so deficient in reading, writing, and ciphering that the town voted to terminate his contract. The visiting and examining scholars by selectmen was a very common procedure on a regular basis, and the inquisitors seemed to enjoy it very much. It might be recalled that special chairs were placed on the schoolroom platform for them to perform their duties.

Next to having the master teach, the pedagogue was often obliged to do numerous other odd jobs in the community, many of which were related to the church.

Among them were:

1. To act as court messenger.
2. To serve summons.
3. To conduct certain ceremonies of the church, perhaps including reading the Bible or the sermon.
4. To lead the Sunday choir.
5. To ring the bell for public worship.
6. To sweep the church, particularly if the church served as a schoolroom.
7. To sing at funerals.
8. To dig graves.
9. To perform other miscellaneous duties.

Although the burdens of teaching and such laborious concomitants appear to have been unreasonable, it is surprising to find that some men spent their entire lives in the classroom. And, it must be understood that there were good and bad teachers. One schoolman in Watertown in 1651 was still active in 1700, thus serving at least forty-nine years at his profession. In another town a Mr. Rogers taught for twenty-two successive years.

He was the most accomplished teacher of his time, not only in English and Latin, but was noted for his unrivaled penmanship.

It is natural to conclude that although some teachers were not very skilled, a man who spent most of his life at the profession would become very proficient. It should be noted that although some very long tenures are documented, the most common service was of only a few years' duration, and was regarded as a stepping stone to some other vocation. One unusual situation involving an older teacher in Malden, Massachusetts, is reported where John Moul was chosen to be the schoolmaster.

He was sixty years old, had spent most of his life at sea, and had never taught a day in his life. His recommendation as a teacher may have been the acquirements which a mariner had gained in the trade of navigation, or the availability of an old man who had little or nothing to do. (And he might have been cheap.)

A few years later they employed a shoemaker of natural ability, but limited education, who had to take lessons from the minister before he could assume the duties of his office.

The shoemaker was a feeble man and had been troubled by many ills; but, apparently the selectmen thought that a sick shoemaker might make a passable teacher. He is said to have been a worthy master, but his value was gauged more on his piety than his ability teach. Yet, this man taught for twenty-five years.

There seems to have been no end to the varied requirements of the teaching profession. One criterion was that a man had to be in dire need of support. To qualify, sometimes the prospective master had to read a chapter in the New or Old Testament, instruct in catechism, and whip boys.

The compensation of the schoolmaster varied a great deal. If he was totally paid in cash, the amount was usually about £30 for one session. Rarely did he get his pay from one source and in the same way. For example, one of the rewards was a town stipend, while he had to collect the rest of his pay from students who attended his classes.

Tuition played a substantial part of support of the schools' (mainly teachers') salaries. The method of paying this tax on the children varied. There were at least six ways: a rate per week; a rate per quarter; a rate per year; a sort of poll tax according to the census of children; and an indeterminate rate according to an agreement between the masters and their parents.

Also, charging students for each subject they were studying was a fairly common procedure.

One of the most frequent methods of compensation was paid by students individually, and the town supplemented this by donations of produce, corn, oats, barley, and wheat. Somehow a standard price was established for such edibles, but the master himself had to use or sell his donations to get his total allotment.

Another way was to accept housing as part of the salary. It seems that most masters were bachelors, so it was very simple for them to live in one room beside or over the schoolroom, or sometimes in a nearby house often otherwise unoccupied and owned by the school district. One example is cited where only a board partition separated the two rooms, so it was possible to hear from either side what was happening in the other room. There are also examples where the master had access to town-owned ground located near the church or school. Of course, the school was frequently "kept" in the church, so the master could use the ground around it, the idea being for him to raise crops on the ground to help pay his salary. The teacher's pay at times also included wood to heat his living quarters.

If the minister served also as a teacher, his ministerial salary was simply increased for his double duty. The prospect of adding a teacher's salary to that of the minister must have appealed to many men, because the teacher sometimes was a full-fledged farmer. On the usually small New England plots he could easily take care of his own in the summer when school was not in session, or when a woman was teaching.

Although not mentioned by authorities on compensation for the schoolmaster, he must surely have served on occasion as a scrivener. There was certainly a sizable number of people who could not write, and many wrote so poorly that they would not attempt to compose legal documents or even usual correspondence. It might be expected that some masters taught writing and were therefore skilled in handling a quill pen. As a matter of fact, teachers may well have made genealogical entries in Bibles or separate accounts which not only included vital statistics, but were colorfully decorated around the edges. Such documents are known to have been made in New England and Pennsylvania and could have been preserved by framing or folding and placing in a Bible for safe keeping. Compensation for such extra duties could have been made in cash, but at best, it was meager dole to keep bones and body together.

The master did have some small compensation—mostly psychic—than grain or money. He was addressed as "Sir" and was usually exempt from military service. He could sit in church with the magistrates, and his wife with their wives. Of course, men sat on one side of the meetinghouse, women on the other.

Finally, the position was described by John Adams in a letter to Richard Cranch, in which he thus grossly burlesqued the pedagogue:

When the destined time arrived, he enters upon action as a haughty monarch ascends his throne, the pedagogue mounts his awful chair and disposes right and justice through his whole empire....

Sometimes paper, sometimes his pen knife, now birch, now arithmetic, now a ferrule, then ABC, the scolding, the flattering, then whacking, calls for the pedagogue's attention.

Dignified in demeanor, strong and forbidding in aspect, harsh, and often cruel in action, the schoolmaster typified the spirit of the age, and

although the colonies were often weary and heavy laden, yet under all their burdens they never wholly abandoned him, but provided for him as one of the pillars upon which their future depended.

As, indeed it did.

Before one leaves the role of the teacher in the New England one-room schoolhouse, some attention might be given to the numerous "dame" teachers who labored there. Although the picture persists in the mind of the author that a "dame" taught in her home, in New England in the eighteenth century she also taught in any other building available to her, frequently, of course, the schoolhouse. Here she gave semipublic instruction under the sanction of the town selectmen, and some assistance from the town treasury; but she depended mainly on tuition individually paid by her students.

Virtually nothing has been said about the professional preparation of these "dames" who conducted the equivalent of primary schools. Their status is particularly puzzling since virtually no girls attended primary schools, nor the advanced grammar schools. Of course, it is known that the ability to read was usually the result of parental guidance at home. Presumably, the "dame" received more than usual attention from her father or her mother. Perhaps she was smart enough or eager enough to become better educated by her own means. She had to be prepared, for frequent contemporary references state that she must be examined and certified if she was to teach in her private or semi-private school.

It is also documented that she taught not only reading and writing to all students, but sewing and knitting to the boys and girls. The few samplers extant made by boys suggest the possibility that they did this type of work in a "dame" school.

The "dame" school probably was started by a woman who was teaching her children in her own home, and soon neighbors would be sending their offspring for instruction in reading and writing. The "dame" rarely coached in mathematics, one exception being a woman who taught oral arithmetic. However, this subject was frowned upon by parents who said it confused the students. The writer can confirm parents' objection for he was taught "mental arithmetic" when he attended his one-room school. At best, it was introduced in the seventh and eighth grades, and then only with limited success.

When the "dame" taught in her own home, any room might serve for the class. Some classes were held in the kitchen so she could attend to other duties there. It is difficult to determine which activity suffered more. Also, barns and other outbuildings were adapted as schoolrooms.

"Dame" school education was particularly well suited to the plan of "moving schools" mentioned earlier in this study. Sometimes the buildings were on the fringes of town habitations; consequently, children often had to walk great distances to reach their classrooms, and so were very eager to get to their lunches at noontime. Some of the food was frequently heated at the fireplace. In some cases, at least, potatoes were roasted and a piece of pork cooked on a stick.

A school presided over by Miss Betty Jermer was located about a mile east of North Common. Only a bridle path passed the door, and when travelers passed by, Miss Betty and her pupils presented themselves and offered their salutations.

Fully documented is the fact that more than one "dame" served one community. In Worcester, Massachusetts, for example, five served the town simultaneously. They were distributed evenly throughout the community so that no child would have a hardship in walking to school. In Meron, in 1732, it was voted to raise thirty pounds and choose "dames" to keep school on the outskirts of town.

Overwhelming evidence exists that "dame" schools were operated also in the summer, particularly when they were semi-public or public. After the practice was established that the "dame" should teach in the summer and a man in the winter, two sessions were arranged. Thus, in very rare occasions, both sessions were taught by a female, and school was generally in session twelve months of the year.

At one place the work of a woman was valued at four and four-fifths months' to one twelve-month session of a male. And in another the tenure of a female was equated with half the value of a male. A case is mentioned when a female received five pounds for teaching, but the length of her service was not given. Yet the instruction by females was paradoxically regarded as better than a man, for the schoolmarms worked at a cheaper rate and were often better organized.

On one occasion a woman was given an additional fee because she had to ride to school on a horse. Although rarely mentioned, riding to school was not an uncommon experience. A female friend of the writer rode a horse to teach, and a special shed was provided to protect the animal from inclement weather. The presence of a shed suggests that more than one person engaged in this practice.

Discipline was on the soft side in "dame" schools. One teacher is known to have tapped scholars on the head with her finger, which was armed with a steel thimble. Another method was to "pin" disobedient children to the apron of the mistress, no doubt a very embarrassing situation as the teacher moved from one place to another among her students.

The quarters in which the "dame" schools were held were equally poor contrasted with those held by men. A "dame" school in New Port in 1798 is described:

The room occupied by the matron teacher and her daughter, Miss Betsy as she was called, was a low, square chamber on the second floor, having no desks, chairs, or other furniture except for teachers and visitors. The children, boys and girls, were furnished by their parents with a seat made of round blocks of wood of various heights.

The early experience of a young student is recalled by Edward Everett, who tells that on his way to a neighborhood school, he had to hold to his sister's apron for protection from the cattle they met en route. The faithful instructress tried to teach him to read before he could speak plainly.

The teacher occasionally acted as a nurse, sometimes keeping a pillow and a bit of carpet for sleepers in a corner of the room where throbbing heads could rest between their struggles with letters in the schoolroom. And they were frequently encouraged to sleep.

Some of the "dames" were colorful figures, especially middle-aged women who dozed in their chairs, took snuff, drank tea, and often something stronger than tea. One student recalls:

At one of these schools kept by Miss Adams, I was daily sent to the grocery store for the teacher at eleven o'clock for a dram of New Englando or Santa Cruz rum, until my mother discovered the practice, and my father called the mistress and forbade her to send me on such an errand.

Frequently the students indulged in antics while the "dame" dozed. They worked off some of their excess vigor by swinging feet which did not touch the floor, and sometimes even tipping over their bench, with resultant laughter and howling. The students assumed they were hurt, but they were happy otherwise in a dull schoolroom. At other moments when the "dame" dozed, they ran around the room with zest and scattered paper from the desks, not infrequently deserting to the outside. When the "dame" awoke from her slumber, she walked through the room switching everyone, the innocent with the guilty. That was considered good discipline.

The "dame" school was eventually merged into a district school. Some final comments:

The public support of school, kept by women, for primary instruction, and free to every inhabitant under the direction of the trustees, though novel, is honorable to the town, and affords a pleasing presage of future improvement.

It has been pointed out that there were reasonably consistent practices in the operation of one-room schools in New England. This condition arose from the unity of most aspects of New England life, including its schools during the eighteenth and early nineteenth centuries.

Another area of importance in the development of one-room schools was in Pennsylvania and surrounding areas. The two dominant groups there were Quakers, who lived chiefly in Philadelphia, and members of the Reformed and Lutheran faiths in the so-called hinterland of Northampton, Berks, Lancaster, Lebanon, Dauphin, and York Counties. Two matters should be mentioned here. First is that the "church" groups comprised the bulk of the population in this back country, their numbers including most of the so-called "Pennsylvania Dutch;" and second, that they were 100 percent Germanic in origin. The "plain" sects—Mennonites, Amish, and Dunkards—were a minority group and had little influence in the development of a culture other than their own in Pennsylvania, and consequently had little to do with general educational policies there. It should be noted, however, that the Amish living in Lancaster County, Pennsylvania, have been released from the mandates of the Public School Act of Pennsylvania, and operate one-room schools today.

Further differences in the operation of the Quaker schools and those of the "church" groups include the latter's demand that instruction be given in the German language, and that the schoolmaster play the organ and lead church congregations in singing. These dual activities required a versatile incumbent.

Considerable data about the one-room school is found in two books, one by Fredrick Livingston, the other by Dr. James Pyle Wickersham.

Probably the most important difference between the one-room schools of New England and those in Pennsylvania is that education started later in Pennsylvania. There a condition of peace existed between the Indians and the German settlers until the time of the French and Indian War. The settlers consequently had fanned out in the countryside, felling trees and starting farms. At first, therefore, great distances separated the families, so the absence of a concentration of prospective students delayed the starting of schools. Moreover, people were involved in making a living, wresting it from the raw country, with little time and attention possible for formal schooling. Their education might be called "home instruction." Man and child were concerned with feeding and caring for cattle, handling a gun, cutting with a sickle, thrashing with a flail, and chopping down trees with an ax. The females had equally important duties.

Research has shown that about seventy-five per cent of the males in the German community were literate and they turned to building schools as fast as conditions permitted. Prior to 1740, no German Reformed schools existed, but by 1760 there were eighty-four churches with thirty-five schools; and new buildings continued to appear throughout much of the eighteenth century. Because conditions among the Lutherans were about the same as in the Reformed group, it might be assumed that they were also building schools or operating classes in churches. However, the fact that both faiths often worshiped in the same church on alternate Sundays suggests that each one was apt to have its own schools.

Attention must now be turned to masters themselves. When schools were first opened, there was a scarcity of teachers and, like their colleagues in New England, many were untrained and unsuited for their profession. However, some men educated in German universities came over with the immigrants, occasionally leaving behind unsavory reputations at home and coming to the New World to start life anew (or continue in their old habits).

Unlike New England where Harvard was founded to train teachers, no university existed in the middle colonies until Franklin got his college started in Philadelphia. The college is known to have had a German department and was well equipped to train teachers for German communities. Bilingual teachers were in great demand in English and German communities.

Few facts are available on the length of sessions in Pennsylvania and on teachers' pay. The fact that many of them did double duty in schoolroom and pulpit suggests that their combined earnings were reasonably good. Salaries of three to six pounds per session recorded in Pennsylvania are low by New England standards. Virtually no statements are made of teachers being paid with produce or grain, although supplying firewood was common; and in many cases the teacher received living quarters free in or near the schoolhouse.

To fully describe the duties and compensations of a master, the following contract is included, the parties being the Lancaster congregation of the Reformed church, and the master Hoffman. Although this contract is not the only source of information, it provides more about the personal and professional life of Hoffman than is at hand from any other source. The time of the contract is included in the first sentence of the document. In addition to duties outlined in it, Hoffman served also as clerk of the congregation.

This contract is preserved in the Harbaugh manuscript collection, and as far as is known, it was in force during the thirty years of Hoffman's service at the Lancaster Church School.

On this day, May 4th, 1747, I, the undersigned John Hoffman, parochial teacher of the church at Lancaster, have promised in the presence of the congregation to serve as chorister, and as long as we have no pastor to read sermons on Sunday. In summer, I promise to hold a technical instruction with the young as becomes a faithful teacher, and also to lead the singing, and to attend to the clock. On the other hand, the congregation promises me an annual salary consisting of voluntary offerings from all the members of the church, to be written in a special register, and arranged according to the amounts contributed, so that the teacher may be adequately compensated for his labor.

Furthermore, I have firmly and irrevocably agreed with the congregation on the aforesaid date that I will keep school on every working day during the entire year, as is the usual custom, and in such a manner as becomes a faithful teacher. In consideration thereof they promise me a free dwelling and four cords of wood, and have

granted me the privilege of charging for each child that may come to my school the sum of five shillings (I say 5 shillings) for three months, and for the whole year one pound (I write £1). I promise to enter upon my duties without fail, if alive and well, on the 24th of November, 1747. In testimony whereof I have written the above document and signed the same with my signature, to remain unchanged for one year from date.

The curriculum of Hoffman's and other schools was a traditional type including writing, reading, and arithmetic. Catechism was added in the summer. However, nothing is known whether it was simply attached to the standard "3 Rs" or offered in addition to the sections.

Contemporary accounts declare that most emphasis was placed on reading principally because book, papers, and almanacs were printed in German, as were also hymnals, Psalters, and Bibles. The importance of the German language is confirmed on many occasions, the immigrants being determined to perpetuate their European culture in their new homeland. Primers and "ABC" books were brought along, but there was never a supply adequate to meet the needs. "ABC" books were among the first ones printed in Pennsylvania. *The New England Primer Improved* was published in Boston in 1770, with a later edition printed by the Sower Press in Germantown. More attention is given to books in the chapter on "School Books."

Due to the wide span of students' ages, discipline was always an important challenge to the teacher. Many were hired because they said they could control the class. Serious and necessary disciplinary action may account for the fact that very few females were hired in Pennsylvania. A long list of rules was read in the first days of the session, and a sizable bundle of sticks displayed to intimidate the unruly young learners. Nonetheless, infractions were common and punishment frequent. Tricks were played on the teacher by placing a board on the top of the chimney and causing the room to be filled with smoke. His lunch was sometimes confiscated along with his bottle of gin, and some ingenious sometimes managed to remove his wig. In certain schools, an average of ten whippings a day and strong epithets such as "dunce," "blockhead," or "rascal" were in frequent use. It was very uncommon for a teacher to control his scholars with love and affection; however, some certainly did.

Among the teachers who achieved fame by kind and gentle methods was Pastorius, who taught in a Friends' school for both sexes. Pastorius was famous for his scholarship and is known to have spoken seven languages. However, the most famous Pennsylvania teacher of the eighteenth century was Christopher Dock, who taught school for fifty years in Montgomery County. Dock was a Mennonite, and his school was patronized mostly by that sect and other plain people. His fame rests largely on his very successful teaching techniques, plus the fact that after his death a book entitled *The Ordinary School* was published, explaining and describing them. He insisted that it not be published during his lifetime, else it appear to be boasting.

Dock also wrote what he called a "Spiritual Magazine," subtitled "A Hundred Necessary Rules of Conduct for Children." Number forty had many different segments with a total of 100 rules. Some of his rules for conduct at school show his kind attitude toward his students. The following are excerpts from that category:

> 51. *Dear child, when you enter the school, bow respectfully and take your place quietly, think of the presence of God.*

> 52. *During prayers, and at the mention of God's word, remember that God speaks to you, and be reverent and attentive.*

> 53. *If you are called upon to pray aloud, speak slowly and thoughtfully, and in singing do not try to outscream the others or have the first word.*

> 54. *Always be obedient to your teacher and do not cause him to remind you of the same thing many times.*

> 55. *If you are punished for your naughtiness, do not express impatience in words or manner, but accept your punishment for your improvement.*

> 56. *At school, avoid this scandalous talking, by which you make your teacher's work more difficult; (do not) annoy other pupils and disturb the attention of yourself and others.*

> 57. *Attend to all that is told, sit up straight, and look at your teacher.*

> 58. *If you are to recite your lesson, open your book without noise, read loudly, slowly, and distinctly, that every word and syllable may be understood.*

> 59. *Attend more to yourself than to others unless you are appointed a monitor.*

> 60. *If you are not asked, keep quiet and do not prompt others. Let them speak and answer for themselves.*

> 63. *Keep your books clean inside and out, do not scribble or draw in them; do not lose or tear them.*

> 64. *In writing, do not soil your hands and face with ink, and do not splatter the ink on the desk or on your or other children's clothes.*

> 65. *When school is out do not make a chatter. In going downstairs do not jump two or three steps at a time, lest you hurt yourself. Go quietly home.*

Dock was a very devoted man, as many teachers of the time presumably were. He said he taught to "erect something in honor of God, and to benefit the young." In his opening exercises all knelt and repeated the Lord's Prayer; and the Ten Commandments were committed to memory. He never chastised children by striking them, but wrote their names on a blackboard with the offense that they committed. As children from different religious faiths attended his classes, catechism was not taught; however, he did quote questions from the Bible and ask children to identify the exact source.

If one of the students found a lost object, he could not claim it as his own until a diligent search was made for the owner. Only after no owner appeared did the object belong to the finder.

Children studied their lessons aloud, as was customary in those days, but during a recitation all had to be quiet. Contemporary accounts mention that there was a buzzing sound in some schoolrooms, and when windows were open it could be heard at some distance from the schoolhouse.

Although Dock could be regarded as a famous teacher because of his kindly methods, he is endeared to antique lovers because he wrote *frakturs*. These renderings of words and design in brilliant color record occasions such as birth and baptismal records. And in the explanation of his technique of teaching, he tells that he made drawings for special students. Some of his works are prized among the most important time and place. Dock's book about teaching techniques is entitled *The School Ordnung.* Written in German, it was translated into English by Samuel W. Pennypacker. Dock was also an author of hymns, some of which are used today.

Other teachers gained fame for different reasons. One of these was Andrew McMinn, who taught at Newtown in Bucks County, Pennsylvania, for forty years, starting in 1772. He presumably had some fine qualities as a teacher, but is notable for wearing a three-cornered hat at all times, chewing tobacco, and defiling the floor with expectorations when the area was within his range.

Although a teacher for only a short time, the famous Baron Steigel officiated in the schoolroom after his unfortunate business adventures. His principal fame lies in his glass factory whose products are highly regarded by fanciers of antiques. For a short time he also operated an iron furnace which cast stove plates with his bust and name across the top.

The famous Benjamin Franklin was not a teacher, but he proposed a concise course of study adopted for certain levels and must have been one of the first men to foresee the important procedure of operating a school on a "grade" organization. Franklin took a dim view of studying foreign languages, and his whole concept was designed to prepare youths to live in their contemporary world. He was joined in this interest by Dr. Rush, who said:

I conceive the education of our youth in this country to be peculiarly necessary in Pennsylvania, while our citizens are composed of many different kingdoms in Europe. Our school of learning, by producing one general and uniform system of education, will render the mass of people more homogenous, and thereby fit them more easily for uniform peaceable government.

A quickening of interest in education in America followed the close of the Revolutionary War. Support for public education was particularly strong in Pennsylvania where a bill was passed in 1834 by the State Legislature supporting grants for education.

Section 1. The legislature shall, as soon as conveniently be, provide a law for establishing schools throughout the State, in such a manner that poor children may be taught gratis.

This article was incorporated into the Constitution of Pennsylvania in 1838 and continued to be the only constitutional provision on the subject in Pennsylvania until 1874.

The law was designed also to help church and neighborhood schools to continue the work started about a century before. It also specified that one-fifth of the cost for operating schools be borne by the state, the balance by a county tax. It further ordered that spelling, reading, writing, and arithmetic form the curriculum. By the 1830s, public education had made gains in Massachusetts, Connecticut, and New York. Between 1827 and 1841 the New York Legislature made grants to academies and seminaries with education departments, but in 1843 the legislators stopped funding these institutions and appropriated money to start a normal school.

Education in Pennsylvania kept pace with New York, where in 1834 the famous law entitled "An Act to Establish Education in Common Schools" was passed.

With increased support for one-room schoolhouses came support for the training of teachers. The first normal schools were at Barrie and Lexington, Massachusetts, in 1839, with the more famous one at Bridgewater in the same state in 1840. Millersville was the first in Pennsylvania in 1855.

The improved training of teachers had a profound influence on certification. However, a kinship with one of the selectmen (school board directors) and a lower pay for the poor teacher continued to obtain employment for many years. Teaching was the only profession open to females, and many of them regarded it as merely a stepping stone to marriage.

A contract with Martin Kellog in New York State shows the contents of such a document in 1843.

Made a contract with Martin Kellog to teach in School District No. 4, five months commencing October 20, 1843. To pay him $12 per month, claiming 24 days a month. Three-fourths of the amount in cash, one-fourth at cash price from Vill. Mfy Store. And to board with every family in the district whether they will have him or not.

The provision for part of the pay in goods was an uncommon feature by that time, because money was of much more stable value than it had been in the eighteenth century. Boarding around was sponsored by the school board and sometimes auctioned to the lowest bidder for the trade throughout the school year.

The following report tells of the experience of one teacher of the same era. He tells that he set out on foot to the place where he was to board and lodge, carrying his wardrobe in a pack on his back, the rest in a handkerchief. The host and hostess were happy to receive him, for they were to be paid sixty-seven cents a week for accommodating him. Their home had only one room, and he slept in a trundle bed which was slid under the big bed during the day.

When school was in session there was frequent change in teachers, many barely getting to know their students. However, the situation was different when the teacher boarded with all the families of his school. Unfortunately, this bred a familiarity which was more a liability than an asset. Another disadvantage was the fact that there was no place for the teacher to privately prepare his work. Some found the practice an inconvenience when they had to pay for "extras."

In New York State there was a definite practice to operate summer and winter terms. Women were usually employed for the summer, for less was expected at that time than of the men in winter terms. Teaching in the summer session was also considered easier than in the winter, hence, the employment of women for those sessions. At one school the same teacher was paid $5.25 a week for the winter term, but only $2.00 a week during the summer.

It is evident that teachers were not paid very well, the result of the fact that men often became teachers because they had failed at some other occupation, and women often because they were merely marking time until the end of the term when they could change jobs or be married.

Conditions in the operation of one-room schools were nonetheless upgraded in the nineteenth century. There was also a corresponding improvement in the preparation of teachers principally because of the establishment of normal schools in most of the states of the Northeast.

Entrance to normal school depended on the result of a written examination, plus a personal recommendation certifying the fine moral character of the applicant. The term was one year, during which they studied the subjects they would be teaching in their one-room schools: geography, arithmetic, orthography, reading, writing, and English grammar. With a fine performance the first year, a student could apply for an additional year, in which time he took advanced courses in his earlier subjects, with additions such as music, principles of piety and morality, and the science and art of teaching.

In connection with each normal school were experimental classrooms where students could for a short time practice what they had learned in their studies. This procedure must have been very successful for the writer practiced in such a program in the 1920s.

In 1891, seventeen percent of the teachers were beginning an average length of tenure from seven to eight years.

In addition to training in the normal schools of the nineteenth century, teachers were further upgraded by attending teachers' institutes, the first one conducted by Dr. Barnard in Hartford, Connecticut, in 1839. Later, institutes were held in New York (1843), Massachusetts and Ohio (1845), and Michigan and Illinois (1846). In the early years, attendance was optional, but their value soon became evident and attendance mandatory. With mandated attendance came payment of salaries, just as though teaching had not been interrupted. In the writer's experience, institutes were held the week before the opening of school in the fall. There were a great many social fringe benefits when teachers got together after going their various ways over the summer months.

The teachers were addressed by leaders in education, recruited largely from the faculties of normal schools and colleges. There were also popular speakers, the writer having heard Will Durant in an institute lecture a long time ago. To keep in step with the old ideas about morality, at least one speaker was a clergyman.

After reading the preceding data about teachers in one-room schoolhouses in the nineteenth and early twentieth centuries, with the knowledge that consolidated schools were coming into prominence, the reader might assume that one-room buildings quickly disappeared. So few of the teachers and buildings seemed to be outstandingly good, replacement seemed inevitable.

However, this was not the case. A new concept appeared on the horizon of the one-room practice that was continued well into the twentieth century. The last one-room buildings in West Virginia were not closed until the early 1970s.

The philosophy supporting school programs is expressed in *Country Life And The Country School*:

The greatest single need for the improvement of country life at the present time, therefore, is for a corps of properly trained country teachers who will enter our existing country schools and, through vitalized teaching and tactful social leadership, convert them into living centers for the instruction of both children and adults and the complete upbuilding of country community life.

This realistic concept creates a new role for teachers in one-room schoolhouses. It was desirable for the teacher to live in his rural community the entire year, so the spending of weekends in a nearby city or town was discouraged. Commandeering of the instructor's time convinced the local people that the teacher not only tolerated them for five days, but enjoyed living among them. To overcome this dichotomy some school districts provided pleasant living conditions for the teacher. Not only were living quarters supplied in the school building, as was frequently the practice in earlier times, but new and attractive houses were built for their teachers. Such good living facilities encouraged male pedagogues to marry and live in the community. However, single women dominated the field in the twentieth century, who had little need for a house and a big garden.

This new concept of rural teaching was nurtured by the establishment of school farms as large as five acres, adjoining the school property. In these farms the rotation of crops and other ideal farm practices were followed, and an orchard was planted with a variety of fruit trees instead of only apples or peaches. Thus, the school was a laboratory for the educating of farmers for the life they were destined to lead.

For this highly specialized type of curriculum, the normal schools established courses to prepare prospective teachers. At one midwest normal school a special rural-type building was erected on the campus and students were "hacked in" from the countryside, an early example of modern day "bussing." This structure served as a model for buildings in nearby rural communities. Another normal school rented a rural building six miles from the campus and transported practice teachers instead of the pupils. Although this setting was the more realistic of the two, it was never widely accepted as better.

It might be pointed out that the new concept of the rural one-room school might have existed only in textbooks, for the writer has no personal knowledge of such school farms in Pennsylvania; however, they might have escaped his notice. In his one-room school all activity took place in the classroom and/or on the playground. There were no adult-related organizations, and although the teacher lived in the community where she taught, she played no major role in social or farming activity. But, she is likely to have taught a Sunday school class, sang in the choir, or played the organ.

6

School Books

A hornbook from
Old Time Schools and School Books.
Courtesy: Dover Publications, Inc.

Of all the paraphernalia used in one-room schoolhouses, none are more famous than hornbooks. The creating of a hornbook is attributed to a scribe who was too lazy to repeatedly write the alphabet and other data on a fragile piece of paper that was later thrown away. Because hornbooks are not reported in any language except English, it is assumed that they originated in England. Although data about early education in Pennsylvania is meager, if German hornbooks had been used there, they would doubtless have been mentioned by one of the authors about that region.

A hornbook consists of a thin piece of wood, possibly eight by three inches, about one-third of which was a narrow handle with a hole through which a leather thong was laced so the hornbook could be hung from the neck or waist of the learner. On the wide portion, a piece of paper or parchment was placed and covered with a thin transparent layer of horn. A narrow band of brass was placed around the edge, and the whole assembly held in place with tacks.

At the top of the paper was printed or drawn the alphabet, upper and lower case letters, followed by an array of vowels, then lines of ab-eb-ib, and other phonetic syllables. The space below was devoted to the Lord's Prayer and, finally, a list of Roman numerals. Hornbooks were used in England from the time of the Reformation until the nineteenth century; however, their fame rests principally on their rarity in America today. Alice Morse Earle mentioned in one of her early books that they had virtually disappeared. This statement brought three to the surface; however, all extant handbooks may not have appeared at that time. Such scarcity is almost unbelievable when an itemized list of one Boston merchant mentioned in 1700:

16 doz. gilt hornbooks 16s.
38 doz. plain hornbooks 19s.

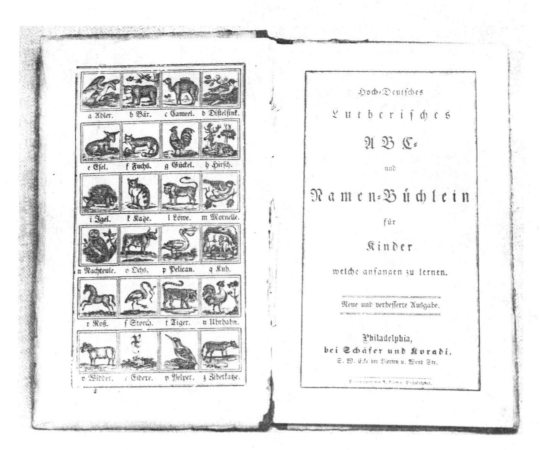

Title page of a German ABC book, probably of the nineteenth century.

In 1899, a copy in a morocco case was sold in New York at the Probasco sale for $147.00. With the present demand for antiques and the inflation rate of 1980, it is difficult to foretell the price one would bring at auction today. The writer has haunted antique shops for forty years and has seen only one in America; however, in 1957 he saw a collection of twenty-one in Burford, England. The famous dealer who owned them said they were the only ones he has owned in his entire career.

Their popularity is attested by the fact that youngsters holding them were pictured by artists. There is even a picture of the Holy Family with the infant Jesus holding one in His hand and being taught by His mother.

Hornbooks were used in the early home and school. The parent or teacher pointed to the letters or verses with a knitting needle or a thin strip of wood, after which the child responded by saying the letter or repeating the verse.

The hornbook was followed by the printed battledore, a double fold of stiff cardboard with a third flap-like section similar to an old-fashioned pocket book. It was bigger than a hornbook and one is illustrated in *Early Schools and School Books of New England.* Each letter is illustrated with an object and a scene. Presumably the combination made learning the alphabet easier, and learning words was another step in the education of the child. Other battledores contain the alphabet supplemented with vowels, a syllabrium, and the Lord's Prayer. Learning was combined with religion well into the nineteenth century.

The next book in the hierarchy of early school books was the primer, also known as the ABC book and catechism. The catechism was a question and answer procedure by a parent, teacher, or the preacher and the child. This comment appears in *Old Time Schools and School Books:*

The earliest books thus named (Primers) contained devotion for the hours, the creed, the Lord's Prayer, a few psalms and some simple instruction in Christian knowledge.

It is thought that the settlers brought copies with them, and excepting the Bible, these primers were the only books in a New England home. Although later printers called them by other names, the original and most famous one is *The New England Primer.* It is not known when the primer was first printed in America; however, the first notice of it appeared in a *Boston Almanac* from the year of the Christian Empire 1691:

Advertisement

THERE IS NOW IN THE PRESS, AND WILL SUDDENLY BE EXTANT, A SECOND IMPRESSION OF THE *NEW ENGLAND PRIMER* ENLARGED, TO WHICH IS ADDED, MORE DIRECTIONS FOR SPELLING; THE PRAYER OF K. EDWARD THE 6TH; AND VERSES MADE BY MR. ROGERS THE MARTYR, LEFT AS A LEGACY TO HIS CHILDREN.

**SOLD BY BENJAMIN HARRIS
AT THE LONDON COFFEE HOUSE IN BOSTON.**

Harris had formerly been a printer in London where he was active in political and religious circles. In 1681 he advanced some ideas that got him in trouble with the government, which apparently ruined his business. In 1686 he appeared in Boston, where he operated a book store and coffee house. Here he published other religious tracts as well as the first newspaper published in America, called *Public Occurrences*.

The *New England Primer* and other books with similar titles held sway in America for about two hundred years. It is estimated that about three million copies were sold; however, all the copies published before 1700 have disappeared. The oldest perfect copy is known to have been printed in Boston in 1735. It is reported that one such copy was bought at a public auction for twelve cents and later sold to a New York book dealer for $2,500.00. This fact was heralded in the newspapers of the country, but later ones were not worth nearly as much, much to the disappointment of people who bought them. Anything later than 1800 is worth only a few dollars.

The covers of the early copies were made of oak wood and covered with blue paper. Neither the back nor the side had any printing, and before the Revolution the frontispiece was an English monarch. After the war, Washington's face was substituted.

The German ABC book used in Pennsylvania was similar in size and function to the *New England Primer*. It was about three-and-one-half by six inches. One in the writer's possession is bound in calf over thin oak boards, and has two brass clamps to keep it closed and intact when not in use. The usual raised bands appear in the spine, indicating the position of cords as part of the binding. On a front fly leaf is written: "This book belongs to Henrick Huber, 1752." Beneath that inscription is written "Johannes Huber, 1776." These two owners might well have been father and son.

A later German ABC book is about the came size as the one previously mentioned; however, it has covers of cardboard. On the front is a replica of Martin Luther with his birth and death dates. He is seated at a table with a quill pen in his hand, presumably writing in the book before him. On the back cover is a drawing of a rooster, suggesting that children get up in the morning when the cock crows. There are only about twenty pages, and the spine is black cloth. This book would not have withstood a good year's use in a public school.

The *New England Primer* and the German examples have alphabets and picture alphabets, doubtless designed to teach the alphabet and reading simultaneously. They also contain easy syllables to be learned by children ranging from two to five or six years of age. They contain a miscellany of religious entries, such as the invocation and the Lord's Prayer. The latter German ABC book has several illustrated stories.

One story accompanies a drawing of a young girl who has upset a pail of milk. The story explains that the girl planned to sell her milk and buy some eggs with the proceeds. From the eggs she would get some chickens which she would sell and use the money to get a green dress, a favorite color of hers. She would wear the green dress to a party. As she imagined her fine appearance, she proudly raised her head, the pail tumbled off, and the milk was spilled. The moral of the story is to be humble and not proud, or dire consequences will result.

Although an exact chronology of books cannot be ascertained at this late date, it is very certain from the dates of books that spellers were among the first used. Their importance is attested by a statement from *Old Time Schools and School Books* as follows:

Advanced readers were in the market in the early years of the republic, but readers for the beginners seem to have been thought unnecessary. The spellers of the forefathers did double duty as spelling books and primers, and were a much more important institution than they have been since.

The purpose of a speller was to acquaint both parents and children with its contents. It was claimed that persons who thoroughly learned the contents could understand "hard"

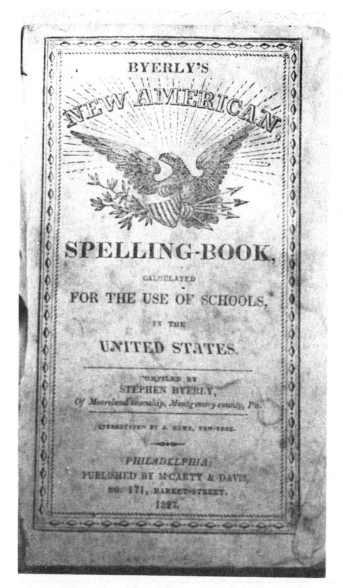

The title page in Byerly's 1827 New American Spelling-Book *displays an eagle—the symbol of the new federated United States.*

could detect the misspelling of any pupil. If this happened, he identified the pupil who made the mistake and demanded that he admit his error. If the error was not acknowledged by the pupil, the teacher kept the whole class until they could recite uniformly and correctly. During such a procedure the hum of the school room could be heard at some distance.

In 1799 appeared one of several spelling books containing eight engravings by the famous divine Isaac Watts. One sketch showing the discarding of old clothing was followed by a number of verses.

> *How proud we are! how fond to show*
> *Our clothes, and call them rich and new*
> *When the poor sheep and silkworm wore*
> *The very clothing long before.*
>
> *The tulip and the butterfly*
> *Appear in gayer coats than I*
> *Let me be dressed fine as I will*
> *Flies, worms, and flowers exceed me still.*
>
> *Then will I set my head to find*
> *Inward adornings of the mind*
> *Knowledge and virtue, truth and grace*
> *These are the robes of richest dress.*

Another spelling book, *The Columbian Primer,* was published by H. Mann in Dedham, Massachusetts, in 1802. This was an attractive book which the author claimed because of its numerous illustrations would be a pleasure rather than a task. Thus it is evident that early authors and publishers were in agreement that "one picture is worth a thousand words."

One of the spellers used in America was a *New Guide to the English Tongue* by Thomas Dilworth. It was reprinted in New England and continued in use there until 1800. In addition to the words for spelling, it contained a short grammar, a collection of sentences in prose and verse, divine moral and historical concepts, and forms of prayers for children. It is evident that morality kept pace with learning well into the nineteenth century.

In *New Guide to the English Tongue* published in Harrisburg, Pennsylvania, in 1811 by John Wyeth, moral sayings are interspersed with spelling words. A sampling follows:

My son, mind the law of God, and you will do well.

Go from the man that will hurt you; and hurt no man thyself.

English words which they would meet in Scriptures and sermons. One speller claimed that "he who hath this book only, needeth to buy no other to make him fit from his letters unto the Grammar School or for an apprentice, or any other private use, as far as concerneth English." A book published by Noah Gruchy in 1718 recommends that the last half hour of the school day three or four days of the week be utilized for drilling in spelling.

Alice Morse Earle describes the teaching of spelling. She tells that the master gave out a word with the blow of his strap on his desk as a signal for all to start spelling a word aloud. The teacher, having done this procedure many times,

All men go out of the way, and do not mind God.

God doth see us in all that we do.

I will sing of the Lord, all the day long.

These are followed by words of four letters, viz. two consonants and two vowels; the latter vowels serving only to lengthen the sound of the former, except where it is otherwise marked. Thereafter are listed words as described:

Babe	*Puke*	*tide*
dice	*mile*	*cage*
fade	*mole*	*cake*
side	*same*	*pike*
wise	*robe*	*gale*
bake	*lice*	*pile*
like	*jade*	*pole*

Lesson seven consists of "Words of four letters, viz. Two Consonants and a Dipthong." This list of words is preceded by moral statements similar to those previously recorded. The words increase in difficulty, the final listing being "Words of three Syllables. Note the accent is on the first Syllable."

ab-so-lute	*ag-gra-vate*
ab-sti-nence	*al-der-man*
ad-jec-tive	*al-man-ac*
ad-mi-ral	*al-pha-bet*
af-ter-ward	*an-i-mal*

Following this list of words are these statements:

Everyday I will give thanks unto thee,
And praise thy name forever.

Great is the Lord, and marvelous;
Worthy to be praised;
There is no end to his greatness.

It might be said here that one expert on the teaching of reading and spelling points out that the constant use of religious comments might well have caused the child to become callous to them so that the precepts were not nearly as effective as the authors and parents thought they should be. However, it took a long time until books became completely secular in nature.

On one page of Dilworth's *New Guide to the English Tongue* is a list of abbreviations. Next is a page of Roman numerals from one to a thousand. This was followed by "A Table of difficult words, according to their Spelling and Pronunciation." From Sheridan's dictionary, "Thereafter was a section of Grammar, and on the same page is Orthography." Orthography was defined: "Orthography teaches the true sound of letters, the right spelling of words, and the division of sentences."

On page 197 are the upper and lower case letters of the Old English alphabet with either the I or the J missing in the upper case, but both appearing in the lower case examples. On page 123 is a woodcut illustrating the fable of "The Kid, the Goat, and the Wolf." Thus, it is evident that a book described as a speller had many other uses, which accounts for their long and wide usage in America. Among the most notable of Dilworth entries is a child's prayer well known to all people today.

Now I lay me down to sleep,
I pray the Lord my soul to keep,
If I should die before I wake
I pray the Lord my soul to take.

A more famous speller was that published by Noah Webster in Hartford, Connecticut, in 1783. Its title reads: *A Grammatical Institute of the English Language, Comprising an Easy, Concise, and Systematic Method of Education, Designed for the Use of English Schools in America. Part 1, Containing a New and Accurate Standard of Pronunciation,* by Noah Webster, Hartford, Hudson and Goodwin, 1783.

This was the first volume of a series of textbooks for the instruction of youth, the second published in 1784 being a grammar, and the third in 1785 a compilation of readings. Because the nation had been at war with Britain for several years, there was a deficiency in the supply of textbooks, and Webster filled the void. The catechism continued to be included in the newer spellers, and in one printed in Boston in 1802, an addition was made to the major title, as follows: "An Appendix contains a Moral Catechism, and a Federal Catechism."

Not only the interruption in the supply of books from Britain during the Revolution, but also the fine quality of Webster's books made them immediately successful. While Mr. Webster worked on his dictionary from 1807 to 1824, his family was supported by the income from his books at a royalty rate of one penny each. It is stated that eighty million were sold previous to

1800, and as late as 1900 thousands continued to be sold annually. Yet in his research for this book the writer did not find one copy of Webster.

It is difficult to understand why Webster's speller was a sensation in the market place, for it was badly published on poor paper and illustrated by crude engravings. However, *The Textbooks for Education* published by The American Textbook Publishers Institute points out that:

When it was first published (speller) it was a declaration of freedom of the American language as against the British. We were then engaged in throwing off the shackles of the British Government, why not her language also? Webster frankly set out to make our language independent of foreign usage; to include our definitions and usage.

Webster's outstanding triumph was that his dictionary is credited with standardizing English as it was spoken in America.

As mentioned earlier, Webster's speller was one of the most influential books published in America. In 1785, just two years after its first publication, it was selling at the rate of five hundred copies a week, and by 1818 about five million copies had been sold. In 1840 the publishing firm of D. Appelton took over the publication and in 1880 they reported that Webster's speller had the largest sale of any book in America except the Bible. As late as 1946, the American Book Company was publishing it and the publishers reported that 163 years after its first publication, 5,000 copies were being sold.

One of the effects of Webster's speller was a craze for spelling, which had not been taught previously as a separate subject. The utility of the book which combined spelling with reading selections became immediately apparent. Spelling exercises became a part of the school ritual. Leaders for two sides were appointed, who chose their teams from the entire school. They lined up in sides and the spelling of words moved from one side to the other, with each incorrect speller being forced to sit down. Eventually the best speller of the school was established, and with the best an "arithmeticer" became the most famous scholars in the school.

Spelling matches were also an important form of winter entertainment. In the evening one school was pitted against one nearby, and it was possible that eventually a county or state champion was established.

All this activity contributed to Webster's success. In addition to being an author, he was a very active man. With the end of the Revolutionary War, a lapse of British copyright laws occurred. Webster was one man who decided something should be done about copyright in America. He conducted a one-man campaign in several states to urge the passing of copyright laws; however, because communication between the states was difficult, a regional "right" was given to publish books. Webster sold "rights" to issue his books to printers (publishers) in Boston, Albany, New York, and Philadelphia, each one being authorized to sell his books. In 1817 one printer, presumably in one of the above cities, paid him forty thousand dollars for a fourteen-year franchise to issue a book in his territory.

Finally, it should be mentioned that Webster was one of the great giants (the other was McGuffey) in textbook history in America. He was enterprising and self-reliant, pursuing his various projects to their successful conclusion. After teaching school in his early years he became a lawyer in Hartford, Connecticut, an alderman in New Haven, a judge in a local court, and a member of the Massachusetts legislature. He came upon the scene when he was needed and he filled his niche with vigor and distinction. As a matter of fact, the writer can well remember when no dictionary was considered equal to the *Webster Unabridged Dictionary*. A local bookstore reports that they have a stock of at least a dozen copies of *Webster's Collegiate Dictionary*.

At the turn of the seventeenth century, basic school instruction was through the hornbook, primer, Psalter, Testament, and the Bible. The only reason for teaching reading was so that the masses could get the ecclesiastical knowledge they were thought to need. Some reading exercises were included in the primers and spellers; however, these lessons were mostly religious in nature. One German ABC book, as noted earlier, included a story of a girl who spilled a pail of milk. The intent was to make the stories interesting by including a woodcut of the affair; however, few adaptations were made to suit the reading materials to the needs and interests of students.

Although books used for reading were probably imported in the early times, the first American reader per se was Webster's with the following lengthy title: *An American Selections in Reading and Speaking, Calculated to Improve the Minds and Refine the Taste of Youth, and Also to Instruct them in Geography, History, and Politics of the United States. To Which is Prefixed Rules in Elocution, and Directions for Expressing the Principal Passions of the Mind*

Being the Third Part of Grammatical Institute of the English Language by Noah Webster Jr., Esq. Hartford: Printed and sold by Hudson and Goodwin. (With their Privilege of Copyright) MDCCLXXXV.

Webster's reader was not as successful as his speller, due to formidable competition from *The American Preceptor* published in 1794, *Being a New Selection of Lessons for Reading and Speaking, Designed for Use in Schools*, and the *Columbian Orator*, published in 1797. These books sold like the proverbial "hot cakes." By 1832 more than six hundred forty thousand copies of the *American Preceptor* had been sold, and more than two hundred thousand of *The Colombian Orator. The Colombian Orator* became important because it was read by the master as a religious exercise at the opening and closing of the school day. Dialogues in it were written by David Everett, a graduate of Dartmouth College, who was famous as the writer of some well-known lines repeated by a seven-year-old boy at a School Exhibition.

> *You'd scarce expect one of my age*
> *To speak in public, on the stage.*
> *And if I chance to fall below*
> *Demosthenes or Cicero,*
> *Don't view me with a critic's eye*
> *But pass my imperfections by.*

The two books were written by Caleb Bingham, who achieved considerable fame as a publisher and as a contemporary teacher. After a number of teaching positions he moved to Boston, where he taught at a school for girls. His curriculum was wider than most, including writing, arithmetic, reading, spelling, and English grammar. His success was instrumental in the establishment of "town girls schools" in which he became a teacher. In 1796 he gave up teaching to open a book store at 44 Cornhill, where he remained until his death in 1817. His appearance distinguished him as a person of more than ordinary stature. He wore a cocked hat, black coat with a white vest and stock, with black silk hose. His winter attire included white-topped boots, and in the summer he wore shoes with silver buckles. He is described in *Early Schools and School Books* as a "gentleman." Another of his outstanding accomplishments was the starting of the Boston Library, which was still in existence in 1904. The first meetings were held in his house and he acted as librarian for about two years.

The utility of readers seems to have become apparent to teachers and publishers; however, it was some time until morality and reading were separated. The previous publications were followed by *The Franklin Primer* which was published in 1802. It was described as:

Containing a new and useful selection of Moral lessons adorned with a great variety of elegant cuts calculated to strike a lasting impression on the tender minds of Children.

The contents are described as "A variety of tables, moral lessons and sentences, a concise history of the World, appropriate hymns and Dr. Watts, and an assembly of Divine Catechisms." The history of the world was based on facts found in the Bible.

The next reader described in *Old Time Schools and School Books* is the *Children's Instructor* published in Philadelphia in 1808. This book included selections from earlier books, having columns of three- and four-letter words and a number of short sentences. The intermixing of spelling with reading was discontinued in this volume, the spelling words appearing at the end of each lesson. There is a lengthy lesson entitled "Description of a Bad Boy."

The next reader chronologically was the *Child's Instructor and Moral Primer* published at Portland, Maine, in 1822. Although direct quotations from the Bible were not used, the contents are studded with names such as Timothy Trusty, Tim Delicate, Charles Mindful, Caroline Modesty, Susy Pertinence, and Cynthia Spindle. The implication of each name is reasonably evident except for Cynthia Spindle.

A Mr. Eeavitt, who obviously thought there was room for one more reader, published *Easy Lessons In Reading* in Keene, New Hampshire, in 1823. He points out that there is an inadequacy in practical readers. He mentions that the Testament has been used for reading but asserts that the contents of his is written in a more familiar style. He also mentions that his book contains precepts and instructive examples for a life of piety and morality, of activity and usefulness.

Another reader was published by a man named Worcester, *A Second Book For Reading and Spelling*, Boston, 1830. Because the contents of his book were geared to the activities of youth, it probably met with considerable success. One interesting insertion in his book was a letter which Lucy Turner wrote to her mother, who was spending a month at the home of Lucy's aunt in Boston. Presumably, this was an example of what not to do.

Mi Deer Mama,

Wen yu cum back, wee shal awal bee pleesed. Evry wun seams dul becaus yu air gon.

Farther ses hee wonts yu too sta longe enuf to hav a gude vissit, butt ie no hee wil bee gladd whenn yure vissit iss ovur.

Jaims gose to skule and ie thinke hee behavis wel. Sarro stais att hom and wurks with mee. Wee awl injoy gude heath.

Doo rite me ay lettur, and tel mee abowt Bosten and ant Wite's foax, and hou soonne wee may expekt yu.

Yure verry luving childe,
Lucy Turner

It is known that before 1850 students in reading and other subjects recited individually instead of in classes. This was the most practical way, for rarely did two students have the same textbook, and if they did, two or three would rarely make the same progress through its contents.

In a recitation, the teacher asked the student to recite, or more likely the student volunteered when ready. With a nod of the head, the teacher recognized the student and the process was started. The child walked down the aisle and with a bow or a jerk, approached the teacher. For beginning reading, the pupil may have been as little as three years old. Such a young child may have been sent to school to relieve the mother of the trouble of caring for the child, rather than to have the child learn. A reading lesson is described in *The District School As It Was.*

*The principal requisites in reading in those days were to read fast, mind the "stops and marks," and speak up loud. As for suiting the tone to the meaning, no such thing was dreamed of in our school at least. As much emphasis was laid on the insignificant **and** or **as**, as on the most important word in the piece. But no wonder we did not always know the meaning of the words, or enter into the general spirit of the composition. This was very frequently, indeed, almost always the case with the majority even in the first class....*

It scarcely ever entered the heads of our teachers to question us about the ideas hidden in the great long words and spacious sentences. It is possible that they did not always discover it themselves.

The author comments about the practice of using the Bible as a reading textbook as follows:

It ought not to be omitted that the Bible, particularly the New Testament, was the reading twice a day, generally for all classes adequate to words of more than one syllable. It was the only reading of several of the younger classes under some teachers. On this practice I shall make a single remark. As far as my own experience and observation extended, reverence for the sacred volume was not deepened by this constant but exceedingly careless use.

At the conclusion of the reading lesson, the student made another slight bow and returned to his seat. Another recitation was started and finished in the same way.

In the middle of the nineteenth century there was a plethora of readers on the American market, most of them being the products of American authors. Although some attempts had been made to gear the books to the needs of the children it remained for the next author to complete the job, and the stage was all set for the second giant in the history of American elementary textbooks, namely, William Holmes McGuffey. McGuffey's position is based on the fact that from 1836 to the teens of the twentieth century, about 122,000,000 copies of his products were sold. In those days it is possible that the sale of his books outstripped those of the Bible.

McGuffey was born in southwestern Pennsylvania on September 23, 1800. When he was about two years old his parents moved to a place in Ohio near Youngstown. At the age of twenty he returned to Pennsylvania to attend Washington College, after which he taught school in an abandoned smoke house near Paris, Kentucky. In 1826 he became a professor at Miami University in Oxford, Ohio, where he married, was ordained as a clergyman, and assumed a prominent position at the college. He resigned his position there and became president of Cincinnati College. When the panic of 1837 caused problems at the college, he became president of Ohio University at Athens, Ohio. Because tax assessments were used to support the college, McGuffey became very unpopular there and in 1845 he became professor of moral philosophy at the University of Virginia. By that time the royalties from his books had stopped, but the publisher favored him with a barrel of "choice hams" at Christmas.

Although William was clearly the major contributor to the series of books named for him, he was not the only author. At one time a wife of one of the publishers contributed to the series, and his brother Alexander also made major contributions. Alexander, who was sixteen years younger than William, taught English for a short time at Cincinnati Academy, but his major work was in the field of law which he followed most of his life, becoming moderately wealthy. After some differences with the publishers, he insisted that his name be removed from the title page of the books in which he was not involved, and his connection with the publishing project was discontinued. The books continued to carry the name of W. H. McGuffey as author, despite the fact that he no longer had any connection with the publishers. It might also be mentioned that after Alexander's name was dropped he did not get any hams at Christmas.

The famous set of *McGuffey's Readers* consisted of a primer and six readers. Although the titles suggested each book was fitted for use in a particular grade, such a conclusion is not true. The numerical title merely referred to their difficulty. The second reader was more difficult than the first and so on up the line. It should also be pointed out that before the middle of the nineteenth century, classes were not graded in one-room schools, each student reciting individually before the teacher as previously explained. Eventually, the McGuffey books were used in the grades suggested in their titles, but that was not the intent at the outset. One student might have been studying reader number six at age fourteen, while another might be using the same reader at age ten. Such activity was determined by the length of time a student spent in school or by the intelligence of individual scholars.

In addition to the McGuffey primers and readers, there were also other McGuffey textbooks. There was a *McGuffey's Eclectic Speller, McGuffey's Eclectic Speaker, McGuffey's Juvenile Speaker*, and *McGuffey's High School Reader*. All these appeared later in the nineteenth century, and since McGuffey's hand was not involved in the preparation of any of them, it is likely that he did not receive any income from them.

Before noticing the contents of the readers, some attention should be given to the way McGuffey became involved in his publications. They were not his original idea, but rather that of Cincinnati publishers named Truman and Smith. They conceived the idea that there was a great demand for school books in Ohio, Indiana, Illinois, and the South. These demands could be filled by their material instead of the books coming from the East. McGuffey was their second choice of author, an invitation which he prob-

William Holmes McGuffey presented a scholarly appearance. Courtesy: McGuffey Museum.

ably accepted very willingly. The publishers drove a hard bargain: McGuffey was to receive a royalty of ten percent on the first one thousand dollar sale of each book, after which all profits accrued to the publishers. After McGuffey left Miami University at Oxford, the publishers cleverly included on the title page that the author was formerly professor at "Oxford." Such deception did not even cause a ripple in the fast-growing western frontier.

After years of publication the owners separated. According to *The Annotated McGuffey*, the Smith member of the firm made two piles of books which the firm published, one containing the McGuffey books, the other the balance of their publications. Smith proposed to Truman that they dissolve their partnership, and each one take a pile. Truman took the big pile, which left Smith with the McGuffey books. Truman's name disappeared as a publisher, and Smith went on to become a millionaire.

The success of the McGuffey readers was not based on their unique contents. Many readers contained the same material, some obviously borrowing from each other. Success was achieved by two means; the first was the clever distribution in the west and the south. For example, during the Civil War outlets in the south were closed, but some plates were smuggled to a southern publisher, the Methodist Book Concern in Nashville. It is not known how the profits were shared with the southern company; however, it was certain that publication was continued, and after the war McGuffey books continued to be sold widely in the south as well as in the north.

The second "ace" of the publishers was the use of the word "eclectic." The concept of the word was imported from Europe where it was widely used in Prussia, Germany, and Switzerland. The word was identified as:

The Eclectic System aims at modifying all the valuable principles of previous systems, without adhering slavishly to the distastes of any master, or views of any party. It rejects the undue prediction from the mere expansion of the mind, to the neglect of positive knowledge and practical application.

It is doubted that many of the buyers of McGuffey's products fully understood the meaning of the statement; however, it sounded like a lucid and reasonable explanation of this strange word.

Two McGuffey books are at hand. One is a primer. The following explanation is in the preface of the volume:

This small volume intended as a first book for children will, it is hoped, be found acceptable as an aid to little learners in their early effort to ascend the ladder of learning.

Simplicity - The lessons contain the most simple words—those with which the ear of the child is familiar. By the combination of these words in easy sentences, connected with pleasing and impressive pictures, it is designed at once to fix attention and to interest the mind, and in this way to make the lesson a medium for imparting ideas to the child.

Progression - A careful progression has been preserved, thus leading the little learner forward, step by step, by an easy gradation which, while it pleases, will at the same time instruct him in the use and meaning of language.

Spelling - Many of the words in the spelling exercise are very often repeated, that the student may frequently spell them. Every teacher is aware that repetition is necessary in instructing young children in this branch.

This book is intended as an introduction to McGuffey's Eclectic First Reader.

This book was published in 1849 by Winthrop B. Smith. It is obvious that certain principles of teaching were mentioned in the preface in case they were not the common knowledge of the teachers. A little advertising was also accomplished by mentioning that the primer was a preparation for *McGuffey's Eclectic First Reader.*

The other McGuffey volume is *McGuffey's Third Eclectic Reader,* published in 1879 by Van Atwerp, Bragg, and Company. The preface explains that this book contains distinctive features of other books, that spelling exercises are included, and in the latter half, definitions are introduced. The latter part was designed to avoid the need of buying a dictionary. Drills are the technique by which the contents are to be learned by the students; they should be explained by the teacher.

The actual contents of readers varied from edition to edition, depending on the most popular ideas of the time. Publication in Ohio suggested that its contents favored the west, but the publisher was smart to point out that they contain no "Sectional" matter. They were aimed at a Protestant white majority of the citizens, they endorsed the temperance movement, and the spread of their contents included subjects such as farming, science, history and biography. Famous American authors included Whittier, Lowell, and Holmes. There were also selections from Irving, Bryant, and Cooper as well as works of English authors Scott, Dickens, Byron, and Tennyson.

By the end of the Civil War the ownership of the McGuffey books changed, the final one being the American Book Company. The two McGuffeys no longer had any connection with the series, but the books continued to sell in large numbers until World War I. With the slow disappearance of the books organizations known as McGuffey Alumni Societies began to spring up in the United States. In 1936 many of these societies merged into what is known as the Federated McGuffey Societies of America, which still meets in Oxford, Ohio, in the home built by McGuffey in 1833. The McGuffey Museum is now housed in that building with an outstanding collection of McGuffey memorabilia. They kindly supplied three illustrations for this publication.

Although arithmetic was mentioned from the very start as an important part of the elementary curriculum in one-room schoolhouses, it was not a mandated subject until Massachusetts passed a law in 1789, which said that in addition to the common subjects arithmetic, English grammar, orthography, and decent behavior had to be taught. At that time the ability to work a complicated problem in arithmetic established a master as superior, and nothing was more likely to get a person a job than to be known as a good "arithmeticer."

The attitude toward arithmetic at about that time was expressed by Rev. Warren Burton in *The District School As It Was.*

At the age of twelve, I commenced the study of Arithmetic, that chiefest of sciences in Yankee estimation. No man was willing that his son should be without the skill in figures. And, if he does not teach him his ABC at home, he will the art of counting at least....

The entering on arithmetic was quite an era in my school-boy life. This was placing me decidedly among the great boys and within hailing distance of manhood. My feelings were consequently considerably elevated. A new Adam's Arithmetic of the last edition was bought for my use. It was consequently covered by the maternal hand with stout sheep-skin, in the economical expectation that after I had done it, it might still help younger heads to the golden science. A quire of foolscap was made to take the form of a manuscript of the full length of the sheet, with a pasteboard cover, as more suitable to the dignity of each superior dimension than flimsy brown paper.

It was always the writer's opinion that the early manuscript arithmetics were used in lieu of a printed book. A statement by Rev. Burton, however, throws a different light on the matter. The situation is described as follows:

My first exercise was transcribing from my arithmetic to my manuscript. At the top of the first page I penned ARITHMETIC in capital letters an inch high, and so broad that this one word reached entirely across the page. At a due distance below I wrote the word ADDITION in large, coarse hand, beginning with a loft A, which seemed like the drawing of a mountain peak, towering above the level below. Then came RULE in a little smaller hand, so that there was a rectangular gradation from the enormous Capitals at the top, down to the fine running-no hobbling hand in which I wrote off the rule.

Burton then continued:

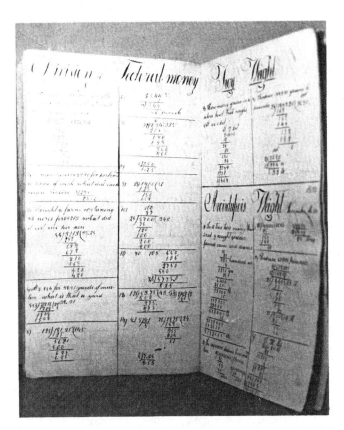

Manuscript arithmetic book. "Federal money" problems indicate that this dates to the nineteenth century. *Courtesy: Schwenkfelder Library.*

I met with no difficulty at first; Simple Addition was as easy as counting fingers. But there is one thing I could not understand—the carrying of tens. It was absolutely necessary, I perceived, in order to get the right answer, yet it was a mystery with that arithmetical oracle, our teacher did not see fit to explain. It is possible that it was a mystery to him. Then came subtraction. The borrowing of ten was another unaccountable operation. The reason seemed to me at the very bottom of the well of science; and there it remained for that winter, for no bucket of thought brought it up to my recall.

Burton continued to be perplexed.

Every rule was transcribed to my manuscript, and each sum likewise as it stood proposed in the book, and also the whole process of figures by which the answer was found.

He states that the next winter he began addition again, and the third year he went over the same ground until he ciphered to the Rule of Three. This procedure was deemed as an achievement for a boy of fourteen, according to ideas that prevailed at the time. He was then fit to fill up the blank pages of manhood and to solve any problems about money that he would meet thereafter.

One of the first printed arithmetic books made in America was by Nicholas Pike of Neburyport. This printing was widely used because it had testimonials of its worth by famous people, including George Washington. It was a massive volume of 512 pages, and presumably had most of the problems popular in the textbooks of the time. It included exercises in addition, multiplication, subtraction, and division, and anyone who advanced to cipher through "Old Pike" was regarded as a genius.

Extracts from the table of contents, indeed, could make any modern mathematician look like a "dummy."

- Extraction of Biquadrate Root
- Pensions in Arrears and Simple Interest
- Barter (This should have been a big chapter)
- Alligation Medial
- To find the years of Indiction
- Table to find Easter from the years 1735 to 4199
- Plain Oblique Angular Trigonometry

It is important to note that in 1786 Congress established the plan for "Federal Money," but it took a long time for it to become the common measure of values. In addition to this decimal system, there were such coins as those from England and Ireland, continental, johannes, pistiles, moidores, doubloons, etc. The computing involved in any business deal was unbelievably complex.

One example of the mysterious mode of arithmetic in Pike's book follows:

Deduct the tare and tret, and divide the suttle by 168, and the quotient will be the cloff, which subtract from the suttle, and the remainder will be the neat.

This matter, of course, was made perfectly clear by the definitions which followed:

Tare is an allowance, made to the buyer for the weight of the box, barrel, or bag, which contains the goods bought.

Tret is an allowance of 4 lb. in every 104 for waste, dust, etc.

Cloff is an allowance of 21 lb. upon every cwt.

Suttle is, when part of the allowance is deducted.

Neat weight is what remains after allowances are made.

Another simple problem found in Pike's book is told in *Old Time Schools and School Books.*

An ignorant sop wanting to buy an elegant house, a facetious gentleman told him he had one which he would sell him on these moderate terms viz. that he should give him a penny for the first door, 2d for the second door, 4d for the third, and so on, doubling at every door, which was thirty-six in all. It is a bargain cried the simpleton, and here is a guinea to bind it; Pray what would the house cost him.
   and. L 2863331153, is. 3d.

In 1796 *An Introduction to Arithmetic* was published by Erastus Root, who omitted fractions but gave special emphasis to the decimal plan of "Federal Money." Later, in 1801 a rival of Old Pike's was published by Daniel Adams. Thereafter came the *Schoolmaster's Assistant* by Nathan Daboll, as well as Walsh's *Mercantile Arithmetic* in 1807. The *Science of Numbers Made Easy* by Leonard Loomis appeared in Hartford in 1816, followed by the *Scholar's Arithmetic* by Jacob Willets in Poughkeepsie in 1817.

By 1821 a new concept in mathematics appeared in Warren Colburn's *Intellectual Arithmetic.* The author utilized some obviously practical problems, all to be done mentally. Most of his problems dealt with every day life, and his publication immediately influenced other arithmetics. The popularity of his book is attested by the fact that in the next fifty years, more than two million copies were sold.

In 1832 the *Franklin* (mental) *Arithmetic* was published in Springfield, Massachusetts. This had problems that make sense today. It is stated that the problems were both interesting and enlightening.

- How many letters in the word JOHN?
- How many in the word SMITH?
- How many letters in both names, JOHN and SMITH?
- How many hands have a boy and a clock?
- A boy played three days in a week, how many days did he work?
- Judas, one of the twelve apostles, hung himself; how many were left?

• Adam was 930 years old when he died, and 130 when Seth was born, how old was Seth when Adam died?

In 1858 *The Normal Arithmetic* by Edward Brooks was published by Sower, Potts, and Company in Philadelphia. Brooks was principal and professor of mathematics in the Pennsylvania State Normal School at Millersville, Pennsylvania. Previously he had authored four books about mathematics; however, this was the first one described and functioned at "mental." This volume was dedicated to:

J. P. Wickersham, A.M.
Principal of the Lancaster County Normal School
as
admiration for his Noble Efforts and
A token in the Great Cause of Popular Education
This Little Volume
is most Sincerely Inscribed by the
Author.

The preface by the author points out that mental discipline (in mathematics) has been poorly taught; however, a great change has been wrought.

A new era has dawned upon the world of science, - the royal road to Mathematics has been so graded and strewn with flowers of reason and philosophy, that it is now full of interest, and profit to the youthful learner; - and one of the most influential agents in this work has been the system of Mental Arithmetic.

The present is a proud period in the history of popular education.

In his suggestions to teachers, Brooks tried to guide their steps in a logical direction. He said:

Common Method. - By this method the problems are read by the teacher and assigned promiscuously, the pupils not being permitted to use the book during recitation, not retain the conditions of the problem by means of pencil and paper, as is sometimes done. The pupil selected by the teacher arises, repeats the problem, and gives the solution, at the close of which the mistakes that may be made should be corrected by the class or the teacher.

The author explains other modes of handling the problems including what is known as the "Double Assignment."

Double Assignment. - By this method the pupil who receives the problem from the teacher, arises, repeats it, and then assigns it to some one else to solve. It may be combined with either the first or second methods. The object of this method is variety and interest.

There was also a method of choosing sides similar to the procedure followed in arranging a spelling match. Two pupils selected by the teacher select others, thus forming two parties in competition with each other. The problems were assigned alternately to the sides, each failure to solve the problem properly requiring the participant to sit down. In this way the champion "arithmeticer" was found for the whole school.

The author also points out that it was important to stand erect in the procedure and not lean against a desk or the wall. Jamming hands into pockets and playing with buttons were also frowned upon. It is finally pointed out that:

An erect and graceful carriage, aside from the relation to health, is of advantage to every lady and gentleman.

Further directions are given concerning errors in articulation, pronunciation, and grammar. Mental arithmetic provided the students with thorough exercise in the performance of all their educational tasks and, as myself, they probably hated it.

Finally, some of the problems posed in the Brooks volume might be included here to give a more complete picture of the proposed activity. The following excerpts are made from Lesson III:

1. *If anything is divided into 8 equal parts, what is one of these parts called?*
2. *What is 1/8 of 24, 48, 72, 88?*
3. *What are 2/8 of 32, 40, 56, 72?*
4. *2/8 of 24 are how many times 3?*
5. *2/3 of 27 are how many times 3/4 of 12?*
6. *A farmer having 48 bushels of oats, sold 4 sixths of them to one man and 1 fourth to another. How many bushels did he sell to each?*

From Lesson LX:

1. *How many times is 2/3 contained in 4?*
2. *How many times is 3/4 contained in 4? in 12?*
3. *How many times is 8/11 contained in 4? in 12?*

51

4. By what method may we derive the results obtained above, without the analysis?

From Section Two, Lesson V:

1. Ella and Kate each have the same number of candies; Ella ate five of hers, and they then had together 22; how many had each at first?

2. The sum of two numbers is 55, and the greater equals 3 times the 1ss diminished by 5; required the numbers.

3. A cow and a horse cost $132; required the cost of each; if the cow cost 2/5 as much as the horse minus 8 dollars.

And, they tried to feed that stuff to me when I was in the eighth grade.

Geography is a subject that might be called a "Johnny come late," as far as the curriculum in the elementary school is concerned. At first, geography books were used as readers and it was some time until it was fully accepted as a school subject. The major protest against it was that studying it took time away from ciphering. Arithmetic was one of the first subjects of the elementary curriculum and it continues to be important even today.

It was not until 1815 that geography was among the subjects needed to enter Harvard, and another dozen years passed until it became prescribed as part of the elementary program in Massachusetts.

The pioneer author of geography textbooks was Jedidiah Morse, who was born in 1761 and graduated from Yale in 1783. A year later his first geography book was published. On the title page of most of his books, his name was appended with D. D. Minister of the congregation in Charlestown, Massachusetts. He had a distinguished career, and a number of his publications were translated to French and German.

There were only two maps in his first book, *Geography Made Easy*. In other pages attention was given to the "Doctrine of the Sphere, Astronomical Geography, and Globes and their Uses." In the description of apparatus used in one-room schools, the globe was invariably included. One can easily imagine a lesson in geography with the students surrounding the globe.

It is mentioned in *Old Time Schools and School Books* that many imaginative tales were picked up from newspapers and included as reliable facts in early geographies. As a matter of fact, it seemed that the more ridiculous the tale, the more likely it would be included in a geography textbook. The following extracts from Morse's books illustrate how unreliable they were.

The Andes, in South America, stretch along the Pacific Ocean from the Isthmus of Darien to the Straights of Magellan. The height of Chimborazo, the most elevated point in the vast chain of mountains, is 20,280 feet, about 5,000 feet higher than any mountain in the known world.

Another fact he dispensed as gospel truth was:

Grey squirrels sometimes migrate in considerable numbers. If in their course they meet a river, each of them takes a shingle, a piece of bark, or the like and carries it to the water; thus equipped they embark, and erect their tails to the gentle breeze which soon wafts them over in safety; but a sudden flaw of winds sometimes produces a destructive shipwreck.

In the general description of the United States, attention is focused on New England, where it said:

A very valuable source of information to the people are newspapers, of which not less than thirty thousand are published every week in New England.

One geography at hand is the *Woodbridge and Willard Universal Geography*, Hartford, 1831. The first section of Modern Geography is the product of Woodbridge, and the second section, entitled Ancient Geography, was authored by Emma Willard. This is the first example found where an author was a woman.

This book has about a half-dozen poor maps with attention again being drawn to the use of globes in the study of geography. In the introduction to the *System of Universal Geography*, the study is defined.

Geography is a description of the earth and its inhabitants, and may be divided into Mathematical, Physical, Civil, and Statistical geography.

1. Mathematical geography is a description of the form, motions, and mathematical divisions of the earth, and methods of representing its surface.

2. Physical geography is a description of the structure and natural history of the earth, including its natural divisions, climates, and productions.

3. Civil geography is a description of the inhabitants of the earth, including an account of their religion, government, knowledge, and arts.

4. Statistical geography is a description of states and empires, with the extent of their population and resources.

The first problem that mathematical geography sets straight is the fact that the earth is round. It tells that if one pursued a course steadily for 24,000 miles, one would return to the point of departure. It also mentions that the earth is flattened at the poles, and the diameter from north to south is thirty miles less than from east to west.

The first paragraph of physical geography sets the stage for the study of this facet by telling:

The general form of the earth is that of a sphere, flattened at the poles; but the surface of its solid body is irregular. In some parts it is hollowed into deep cavities which are filled with water of the sea; in others, it rises above the level of the water and forms land whose surface is diversified by mountains and valleys.

Civil geography starts with a discussion of the races of men, enumerated as European, African, Asiatic or Mongolian, American, and Malay. Among the subjects discussed under these headings are: Language, Government, Religion, Education, Agriculture, Roads, and Commerce. Probably the most interesting discussion of religions was a very pertinent matter to the world in 1980.

There are two principal sects of Mahotans, who differ concerning the right of succession to Mahomet. The Sheas or Shiites, who are chiefly Persians, and the Sommite who embrace the inhabitants of east Persia, Arabia, Turkey, and the independent Tartary.

Under the heading of Literary Institutions is an interesting comment about education in Europe compared to college education in the United States.

The college and universities of Europe differ materially from those in the United States. They are rather a place for study for those who wish to acquire knowledge. Scarcely any control or care is exercised over the character and conduct of the students and their efforts are chiefly voluntary.

The final division of *Universal Geography* is under the heading Statistical Geography. The first section deals with "National Power." It is related that Great Britain holds the highest respect to knowledge, arts, and enterprise and possesses powers which no other nation can control. Her commerce and naval force have enabled her to exert influence in every quarter of the globe. France, Austria, and Prussia also belong in the first class of powers. The influence of Russia is also great, although less than the others enumerated. In Asia, Russia is the most important power, with the Chinese empire next in extent. The small but populous Japan seems possessed of ample means of self-defense, but at that time had no communication with its neighbors.

Thereafter follows a discussion of the United States, with Pennsylvania receiving the most comment. It is pointed out that the agriculture of the state is superior to any in the country, and stands very high in the production of manufactured articles. Harrisburg is described as the seat of government, pleasantly situated on the banks of the Susquehanna River. There is also a description of Lancaster and Easton. The various territories are also mentioned. The balance of the descriptions are of other regions of the world, with maps of Great Britain, and progress of the Roman Empire.

The section about Ancient Geography is more history than geography. It is implied by Emma Willard from other important stand works of geography, to which is added Problems of the Globes. Miss Willard explains:

The Systems of Ancient Geography which I have examined were not adapted to my peculiar views. I therefore arranged one for my pupils, the same which forms the basis of that which is offered to the public....

With respect to the succession of events, without particular care to prevent it, the study of Ancient Geography will tend to confuse instead of enlightening the learned....

The only portion of the earth known to the ancients were those lying around the Mediterranean Sea, comprehending the southern and largest part of Europe, northern Africa, and southwest Asia.

A very poor map illustrates the parts discussed, and shows Europe to be very small, Britain hardly noticeable, and most of Asia occupied by Scythia, or what is known as modern Asiatic Russia. Considerable wordage is given to descriptions of Athens, Rome, Alexandria, Herculeaum, and Pompeii, with a small map of Pompeii.

Mythology receives some attention as does Sacred History, subtitled "View of the Journeys of Our Saviour." It is noted that in A.D. 28:

In the first year of His ministry, Jesus went from Nazareth to the river Jordan, where he was baptized by John. Thence to the Desert of Judea where he fasted forty days, and then to Bethany beyond Jordan or Bethabara, where John was.

The final part of Ancient Geography is by W. C. Woodbridge and deals with the construction of maps. The terms celestial and terrestrial globes are defined, and thereafter is enumerated the most important parts of map making, such as Two Poles, the Brass Meridian, the Wooden Horizon, the Hour Circle, and the Mariner's Compass.

Geographies increased in number and importance by the middle of the nineteenth century, a number being available for use in one-room schools. Among them was *Geography of the*

THE

FIRST BOOK OF HISTORY:

FOR CHILDREN AND YOUTH

BY

THE AUTHOR OF PETER PARLEY'S TALES

WITH SIXTY ENGRAVINGS AND SIXTEEN MAPS.

Revised Edition

BOSTON:
JENKS & PALMER.
NEW YORK:
COLLINS, BROTHER & CO.
1844.

Productive System by Roswell C. Smith, A.M., published in New York in 1854. The first part of the book deals with questions and answers.

Q. What does a view of these divisions (land and water), especially the ocean and its wonderful properties, teach us?
A. The wisdom and goodness of the Great Author of all things.

Despite the fact that the above quotation deals little with geography as it is known today, most of the book does describe the various regions of the earth, starting with the hemispheres and finally getting down to the states and other major divisions such as Greenland, New Britain (Canada), Bermuda, the West Indies, etc.

As in the previously mentioned geography, there is one section entitled Ancient Geography.

Ancient Geography relates to that portion of the earth which is known as the eastern hemisphere. The knowledge which the early Greeks possessed of the countries around them was very limited and imperfect, and their notions about the form and divisions of the earth seem to us very ridiculous.

Generally speaking, the maps in these geographies were very poor and not very numerous. The persistent use of globes is implied. There were, however, frequent scenes of cities and the countryside.

The final textbooks to be discussed in this survey which were used in one-room schoolhouses are histories. In 1822 Rev. C. A. Goodrich published his history, which for a long time surpassed all rivals in popularity. It is reported that within a dozen years, fifty thousand copies were sold. In 1832 a school *History of United States* was published by Noah Webster. This was followed by Butler's *History, Sacred and Profane, From the Creation of the World, To the Year 1818, of the Christian Era.* This one was filled with religious concepts and had many full-page copperplate engravings, one of which was entitled, "Conflagration of Moscow." Rev. Robbins'

In the realm of school textbooks, history books are not common. History was late in coming to the curriculum of the one-room schools.

book, published in Hartford in 1835, tells the scriptural story of creation, about 5,829 years ago.

Pictured on the previous page is the *First Book of History: For Children and Youth by the Author of Peter Parley's Tales*, with sixty engravings and sixteen maps, published in Boston by Jenks and Palmer in 1844. The author points out in the preface:

In preparing it (the book) two things have been in view. In the first place, it should be useful; and in the second place, to make it useful it must be interesting.

The publishers launch an attempt to make history a more widely taught subject in the schools. They point out that the subject is well adapted to school use; however, many textbooks have been merely a chronology of uninteresting dates. This complaint was common when the writer studied history in the early part of his school career, and the criticism was well-founded.

As many books of the period, this one is small. It deals with the western hemisphere with the suggestion that if it meets with success, one will follow dealing with the eastern hemisphere. At the end of the book, contrary to the comment about history books, are four pages of recommended facts to be "riveted" in the minds of the students.

Considerable drama is described in the various battles of wars, and there is an obvious attempt to arouse the patriotism of the students. Comments about the Revolution seem to be generally true with the mention that France came into the war as an ally. After the war of independence, the nation took her place among the nations of the world.

In 1854 *The First Book of History Combined With Geography* was published. The contents of this book are limited to the western hemisphere and it is well illustrated with **colored** maps.

It (the book) contains nineteen maps, newly engraved upon steel, and colored, which contain the names of all the places referred to in the work, and those maps are inserted in connection with the states and countries they represent.

One would think that by the time this book was published the two subjects of its contents would have been treated separately; however, it does appear that the combination offers a ready way to learn both of them.

The students of one-room schools not only supplied their books, but also other paraphernalia needed for their school days.

Having previously had promise of writing this winter, I had made all the necessary preparations days before school was to begin. I had bought me a new birch ruler, and had given a third of my wealth, four cents, for it. To this I append-ed by a well-twisted flaxen string a plummet of my own running, whittling, and scraping. I had hunted up an old pewter inkstand....I had succeeded in becoming an owner of a penknife, not that it was likely to be applied to its appro-priate use that winter at least....I had selected one of the fairest quills out of that enormous bunch.

Rev. Burton prefaces these comments with the statement that his mother folded into shape a writing book (manuscript) and covered it with heavy brown paper as thick as sheepskin.

On arrival at school the first day he took a seat higher in the hierarchy than he occupied the year before, and at the proper time handed the master his paper and quill. The teacher "set" a copy for him to reproduce, which was a straight line. This he thought simple, but before trial he looked at the product of the boy sitting next to him, who had already tried his exercise. Encouraged by his failure, Burton proceeded with his own work.

He reports, "Never shall I forget the first chirographical exploit of my youth." He had a shocking experience in viewing his work. The marks looked like ribbons fluttering in the wind, and some were as rough as the teeth of a saw. His pen diverged from right to left, crooking all the way, with as many zigzags as could be done in the given distance. In the afternoon, another copy was "set" by the teacher which, unfortunately, ended in puddles of ink.

Later his work included the first elements of "m" and "n." On the fourth morning he finished the letters. In this way, he went the entire way through the "small" alphabet. Next came the capitals, which looked like capital offenses.

Burton then explains that some few teachers spent a few minutes going around to see that the students held their pens correctly. There was an excuse, however, for not doing that, for in the process a number of students sitting at the long desks had to be inconvenienced. There was rattling and fussing, and sometimes ink-wells were upset.

Some of the teachers took the manuscripts home with them to "set" the copy the night before; however, they were not paid for work outside the school building, and only a few teachers did it.

One of the most critical parts of writing was the making of pens. That is the reason for buying a penknife, but the teacher cut and repaired the pens and the knives carved the desk. Burton's teacher did have a session of pen-making, but to his great regret, he missed it.

Two more subjects were in rare cases a part of the one-room school curriculum, namely, music and art. There were no books for these subjects and each teacher made his own plans. In some cases the subjects were entirely neglected. They would have appealed to the students more than the subjects discussed. There was not much fun in the old schools, and maybe there is too much today.

A manuscript book plate for a music book, done in Lancaster County, Pennsylvania, in 1815. Courtesy: Lancaster County Historical Society.

7

Teaching Apparatus

The reports made by various superintendents of schools about the year 1850 emphasize the fact that very few schools had any apparatus to demonstrate scientific concepts to their students. As a matter of fact, some were lacking what might be regarded as essentials for the operation of a successful teaching program. This lack can be easily understood, for at that stage of development, the school's major struggle was to supply a very minimal education.

The time of visual aids had not yet arrived, and it had not arrived at the one-room school I attended in the 1914 to 1922 era. The absence of such objects can be further explained by the fact that in the early nineteenth century teachers needed less than a high school education and they were not trained to use apparatus. One teacher's best recommendation for employment was the fact that she was from Massachusetts, a state regarded as a leader in public education. It is difficult to believe that she could not write a coherent sentence, and had an advanced student in her school write for her.

Furthermore, the description of the early schools gives the distinct impression that there was no room to store apparatus. The schoolhouse consisted of only a bare room with no closets or storage space.

In 1855 the author of *Pennsylvania School Architecture* commented about a new generation of teachers:

A new and better order of professional Teachers, trained in the duties of their profession, whose whole time and talents will be devoted to the cause of education, are coming on the stage, and will demand their appropriate tools to carry on their work.

The following data about apparatus was taken from books of the mid-nineteenth century.

In the view of teachers and school committee members, the blackboard was the most useful object in a schoolroom, next to desks and seats. Literature suggests that blackboards were a rarity in the early schools, and some schools in the nineteenth century did not have any.

The first ones were made by carpenters who built the school structure. Wide smooth boards without knots were joined along their edges, with cleats on the back to help keep the joints together. The heat of the schoolroom would make the joints open unless both sides of the wood had been painted. To keep the boards together more securely, the entire unit was placed in a frame before fastening it to the wall. The frame went the whole way around the blackboard, with a trough on the bottom to catch the dust from the crayons and to serve as a temporary resting place for the wipers (erasers). The smoothed surface was painted black with a dull paint.

Another method of making a blackboard was to paste paper on the plastered wall of the schoolroom and cover it with the following recipe:

Lamp-black and flour of emery mixed with varnish. No more lamp-black and flour of emery should be used, than are sufficient to give the required black and abrading surface; and the varnish should contain only enough gum to hold the ingredients together and confine the composition to the wall. The thinner the mixture, the better. The lamp-black should first be ground with a small quantity of alcohol to free it from lumps. The composition should be applied to the smooth surface with a painter's brush. Let it become thoroughly dry and hard before it is used. This kind of surface, if properly made and used, will last for several years.

An alternate method of making a blackboard was to use plaster, as follows:

As a substitute for the painted boards, it is common to paint a black section of the plastered wall when covered with a hard finish (i.e.,

57

plaster of Paris and sand), or to color by mixing the hard finish with a sufficient quantity of lamp-black, wet with alcohol, at the time of putting it on. The hard finish, colored in this way, can be put to an old wall as well as a new surface. Unless the lamp-black is wet with alcohol or sour beer, it will not mix uniformly with the hard finish and when dry, the surface not being a uniform black, will present a spotty appearance.

A portable blackboard could be made from a panel of wood covered with canvas and painted with three or four coats of black paint. Henry Barnard, in his *School Architecture*, suggested that letters be written on one side and a musical scale on the other, the first to be used in teaching penmanship, and the second, a means of informing scholars about some fundamental matters relating to music. This panel was to be mounted in a rigid frame with rollers so it could be conveniently moved from place to place.

About 1850, there were some new ideas about blackboards, for then the first ones made of slate were being installed. These big slates cost only two or three dollars each, but that price was considered too expensive for an ordinary classroom. Of course, smaller slates were considered an absolute necessity for each student to have, one on which he could draw or cipher when not otherwise occupied. To withhold a slate from any student because of the fear that it might be broken was regarded as miserable economy. The saving of wear and tear on books would easily compensate for any loss in broken slates.

The small slate was to be framed in a good oak frame, fastened tightly around the corners by a band of sheet iron or a wire. Neither the wire nor the iron should project beyond the thickness of the frame or it would scratch the desk. The writer remembers slate frames that were bound with an attractive red cord which not only made the edge safe, but added to the attractiveness of the unit.

Some desks had a facility for the storage of the slate when not in use; however, no such devices are evident in the drawings of desks and seats. It was found that if students started early in their school career to use individual slates, they were more likely to be successful when they were placed at a large one on the wall.

Of course, a special writing tool was needed to write on the big blackboards and slates. Slate pencils were used for the small individual slates. Either because of a tight economy or because chalk was not available, most of the books gave directions for making chalk. The following directions were given for making a very satisfactory marking device:

To make crayons or chalk, take five pounds of Paris White and one pound of wheat flour, wet with water, knead it well, make it so stiff that it will not stick to the table, but not so stiff as to crumble and fall to pieces when rolled under hand.

To roll them out to the proper size, two boards are needed, one to roll them on, the other to roll them with. The first should be a pine board three feet long and nine inches wide. The other should be a pine board a foot long and nine inches wide, having nailed on the under side, near each end, a slip of wood one-third of an inch thick, in order to raise it so much above the under board, so that the chalk or crayons, when brought to their proper size, may lie between the boards without being flattened.

The mass is rolled into a ball and slices cut from it about one-third of an inch thick; these slices are again cut into strips four inches long and one third of an inch wide, and rolled between the two boards until smooth and round.

Finally, the round crayons were laid on one of the boards (four inches wide) compactly, with the uneven ends projecting beyond the edge of the board. Next, the ends were cut so that all were exactly the same length. The filled board was then laid in the sun, in hot weather, or in the winter near a stove or fireplace, for about twelve hours. When thoroughly dry, the chalk was ready for use.

A wiper made for the large blackboards was made by cutting a piece of wood about eight inches long, five inches wide, and one inch thick. To this board a piece of sheepskin was nailed, wool side outward. If a handle was provided, this object would serve for a very long time. A sharp-edged wiper of wood was used to skim off the unwanted dust. In my one-room school the wipers (erasers) were made of felt and were cleaned by patting them against each other during the recess period or after the close of the school day.

The following apparatus is not given according to its importance in a one-room schoolhouse; however, maps would certainly rate very high in importance. One authority said that the best maps were outline maps that did not have any names on them. Presumably, the children would pay attention to any lessons about maps, for they could not refresh their memories by referring to them at a later time. The same man also writes that maps should be artfully colored and hung on the walls of the schoolroom for their decorative and informative value. He recommended that there should be no fewer than ten maps available for each school, including maps of America, Europe, Asia, and Africa, maps of the Eastern and Western Hemispheres, North and South America, the state of Pennsylvania, and the county and township in which the school was located. They should not be folded unless absolutely necessary.

Although many school districts could not afford to buy one, a "magic lantern" was high on the priority list. It consisted of a tin box with a door on one side for inserting the lamp, a lens on another side, and a chimney on top to discharge heat and smoke. The fuel for the lamp was kerosene. Slides were inserted between the box and the lens so that the picture would be projected on to a screen placed at the proper position and distance from the lantern. These pictures would be sure to fascinate children. In my childhood I had one, and it was always a special occasion when I was permitted to light the lamp and show pictures.

The ones used in the schools seem to have thrown light on every subject imaginable. Among them were systems and suns, constellations and comets, Adam and Eve, David and Goliath, and the prodigal son. Closer to home were pictures of Naples and Venice, Niagara Falls, and New York City. Subjects included natural history,

botany, and various kinds of animals. The price of these instruments varied from five to one hundred dollars.

The inkwell was an indispensable part of the desk. When it stood on the desk, it was very likely to be upset when used, so a hole was cut in the desk into which the well was fitted. In the early days, all writing was done with quills. A teacher's value was sometimes placed on his ability to cut or sharpen quills and re-cut them after they were damaged. In the earliest days ink was a scarce commodity, for each family was its own ink manufacturer, and some parents were negligent in this matter. Homemade ink was either made from ink powder imported from Britain or New York, or it could be cooked from a combination of swamp maple bark and copperas. Steel pens came into general use about 1850 while pencils were introduced as early as 1820 but did not become common until about 1850.

Although geography was not one of the first subjects taught, by the middle of the nineteenth century globes were available and were doubtless used by some of the progressive teachers. Globes were mounted on stands with an arrangement that allowed them to turn. There were two types: the terrestrial and the celestial. The terrestrial showed the location and comparative sizes of the hemispheres and the oceans. They also showed the equator, meridians, parallels and poles, latitudes, longitudes, axis, and zones.

Besides having difficulty in grasping the idea that the earth was round, the students were particularly frustrated by the markings mentioned. One globe was somewhat realistic—after examining the hemispheres, the student could open the globe in halves and see pictured on the flat surfaces within the circular hemispheres shown on the surface of the globe.

The celestial globe facilitated learning about the heavenly bodies and helped the teacher to impart some simple concepts about astronomy. Globes were usually sold in pairs, a small one in a case costing about six dollars;

large ones cost more in proportion to their size.

One medium not commonly regarded as part of the apparatus for a one-room school was an omnium gatherum, or more simply, an object box. Because the pupils were not likely to travel far from their homes, the teacher tried to have examples of many objects unfamiliar to them, in a box conveniently stored so she had easy access to it, and, at times, could use the contents in her teaching.

Sometimes a lesson centered around objects in the box. Samples might include: silk, muslin, flannel, oilcloth, felt, drugget (what is that?), bricks, pottery, china, glass, iron, steel, copper, lead, brass, pewter, a piece of type, a ring, a needle, a pin, a button, steel pens, unusual paper, parchment, leather, morocco, kid, buckskin, cocoon, coffee, cinnamon, wheat, oats, barley, buckwheat, sponge, shells, different kinds of wood, etc. Obviously, these items could be useful visual aids for the teacher and in case they were not supplied, she was able, over the years, to build up a store of her own.

Cards and pictures could be brought in to fill in for objects and subjects not easily stored in a box. Cards might have words and designs that could be copied, and when not in use, hung around the schoolroom as ornaments. The subjects could also be animal and nature forms. Some were white lines on a black background and were called chalk drawings.

One interesting piece of equipment was necessitated by the condition of the unpaved roads which the scholars traveled to school. As a matter of fact, the schoolyard became a sea of mud in the spring of the year so that the shoes of pupils could not help but to accumulate a covering of mud.

It was suggested in 1855 that a small portion of the schoolyard immediately in front of the door and steps be laid with a brick or plank floor. By stamping their feet on this hard surface pupils could remove some of the mud; however, that which remained had to be removed by a scraper. More than one scraper was recommended. Since most of the students came to school at about the same time, one scraper would not have sufficed. At least one for the boys and one for the girls was suggested. Lacking adequate scraping resources, the pupils would enter the building tracking mud on the floor. In this way, dirt would be ground into the floor by the pupils walking around in it, thereby creating a very unsatisfactory situation.

As a connoisseur of work in wrought iron, the writer is curious about the beauty of the scrapers. Made by local blacksmiths, the scrapers frequently were fancy as well as very functional. The vertical members of the scraper might terminate in scrolls with interesting designs filed on the bottom edge of the horizontal part. Of course, if scrapers were too attractive, they might be stolen by mischievous students or adults.

After most of the mud was removed from the shoes by the scraper, an outdoor and indoor mat finished the job. If the students thoroughly cleaned and dried their shoes, there would be less danger of getting colds and other discomforts caused by wet feet. In addition, there would be less dust in the schoolroom caused by drying out of the mud. Circulating dust could pollute the air of the classroom and it could settle on the desks and seats, not to mention the books and slates.

At least one mat was needed just inside the front door, or on the porch if there was one. If the teacher knew how to make a corn husk mat, she could easily teach the larger students how to make them and a supply of mats could easily be provided. Mats were probably made of other materials also; however, the writer cannot suggest the materials or the means to make one. Probably the simplest solution was to use odds and ends of carpet. Considering the fact that mats would become very dirty in a short time, some method of cleaning them had to be devised. A clever teacher would probably assign this work to older students. As the community surrounding the school became more aware of the needs of the schoolroom and its facilities, the adults would probably attend to some of these details.

There were suggestions for installing a facility for draining umbrellas, although it is not likely that many students used umbrellas. The simplest recommendation was to cut a barrel in half and place the halves in the corners of the room to hold the umbrellas. A more sophisticated device was a watertight trough one foot wide and one foot deep mounted on four legs about ten inches long. About a foot above the top edge of the trough, a guard or rail might be constructed on which the umbrellas could be leaned. There should be a hole in the bottom, closed with a cork, so the water could be periodically drained. The device might be painted the same color as the interior of the building, thus becoming an attractive addition instead of an eye sore.

If there was a well and an adequate supply of water, a wash basin in a stand was suggested. Pupils often came to school with faces unwashed and hair uncombed. To keep a neat and healthy school, such pupils had to be washed and combed before they sat down with the other students. Because in a rural area it was impractical to send pupils home for such refinements, facilities had to be maintained in the school. Of course, soap and towels were needed which the teacher might have to supply if the community was unwilling to do so.

Most of the schools were in the countryside at distances too far for the pupils to go home for lunch. As pointed out earlier in this study, a facility for storing lunches was often not available. There were a variety of ways for keeping lunches safe until the noon-day meals. The simplest solution was to have a shelf on which lunches could be placed. When box-like desks came into vogue, a pupil could keep his lunch in his desk, thus making sure that his food would not be disturbed by another student, or by dogs or hogs as mentioned earlier.

The most sophisticated method recommended was to have a lunch closet with a lock and key to secure the contents until needed. The key might be entrusted to a mature student who could control the movements of the other scholars; otherwise, it stayed in the possession of the teacher. One closet illustrated has a very attractive design consisting of two sections, the lower section with paneled doors, the top doors being filled with glass. It is not likely that many Boards of Directors would have supplied such a useful and attractive object; however, as schools improved in the last half of the nineteenth century,

such a facility might have become available. Lunches were deposited in the desks of pupils in my one-room schoolhouse.

One authority suggested that in order to control the quantity of light, the schoolroom should be supplied with venetian blinds. These could be managed to prevent bright direct sunlight from falling on books and slates. The evident lack of more important appendages suggests that venetian blinds might have been pretty far down on the priority list of school boards; however, the modern slang impression of "it won't hurt to try" might have been usefully applied. Nevertheless, some device for controlling the light was necessary, and the most frequent solution was to use blinds and/or curtains. Blinds which rolled up on a roller were most likely to be provided by the Board of Directors, but the teacher with the cooperation of the students might have supplied curtains. In the eyes of visiting superintendents, windows needed much more attention than they were getting in the first half of the nineteenth century.

After reading the comments by superintendents about the shabby conditions of schoolhouses and the indifferent housekeeping within, it is possible they reported the worst and most neglected conditions. There must have been some schools in tip-top condition, with teachers who were sensitive and informed about good school practices. Unfortunately, they were not reported as frequently as the bad examples.

One of the minor members of the apparatus family was an abacus. Its usefulness in teaching rapid small computations in mathematics is very obvious. An abacus consists of a frame of wood on which twelve wires were mounted, each wire having a certain number of wooden balls. Instead of counting on their fingers as beginning students are apt to do, pupils could compute on an abacus as the teacher shifted certain numbers of balls from right to left, or visa versa, on the mounted wires. This little instrument was a very useful device for the teacher to use. It is likely that many schools had at least one since they were easy to store, and reported to cost only one to five dollars each.

A small learning accessory that could be put into the hands of the pupils was called geometric solids. Since there was little danger of their getting broken or otherwise spoiled, it was safe for the students to handle them. They were made of wood in forms such as cubes, cones, prisms, spheres, spheroids, cylinders, and triangular sections. A foot rule and a yardstick could easily be added to teach the concepts of measurement. A teacher might also bring in liquid and dry measures. Because most of the students lived on farms, such concepts were important to them.

Another assemblage of small mechanical devices fits into the category of "mechanical powers." Children from the farm were constantly being confronted with the practical application of such phenomenon, which, if thoroughly understood, would make life more successful. Apparatus such as that illustrated would in a short time give the students a good practical knowledge of the principles of mechanics. The set should include simple and compound levers, a wheel and axle, the pulley (fixed and movable), the inclined plane, the wedge, and the screw. Such sets were available from commercial suppliers for from five to one hundred dollars.

A tellurian, or season machine, was also recommended for use in a one-room school. Its operation was a bit more complicated to understand than the mechanical powers and geometrical solids. Its purpose was to help the student to understand various parts of the solar system, the revolutions of the moon around the earth, and the earth around the sun. Although this information appears to be a matter of astronomy, it was considered advance geography, particularly as its function helped the scholar to under-

derstand certain phenomena which influence the manners and customs of people living in different parts of the earth. For example, the "long night" is experienced by people who live in the northern part of the Scandinavian peninsula.

With only a few exceptions, the apparatus described thus far was reasonably simple and easy to understand. However, the middle of the nineteenth century ushered in a period of national growth and mechanical inventions. Students were hearing about electricity, and because of the uses of steam, people were excited about the steam locomotive. It might be expected that innovative educators of the period would want to inform the students about the various mysterious phenomena. This was done by using a variety of miniature scientific equipment.

The demonstration of a simple electrical apparatus was recommended to keep the students in constant wonder and delight. The operator seemed invested with magical supernatural power. By turning a crank he could call this invisible power into action, direct its energy and control its force. It could create sparks that crackle or make one's hair stand on end. It is very obvious that such a machine would thrill the students and provide an enthusiastic conversation at the supper table at home.

A subject similar in importance to electricity was pneumatics (pertaining to, consisting of, or containing air). A comment about the apparatus stated that "many beautiful and interesting experiments may be performed with an air pump. These experiments demonstrated clearly and practically some facts which, to the uneducated, would seem paradoxical."

For example, to prove the air is the means of transmitting sound, a bell was placed under a sealed glass container, and with a pump the air removed from the enclosure. The mechanical apparatus supplied with the unit was used to strike the bell with a clapper, but no sound would be carried outside the assemblage. After the air was replaced within the container, the sound of the ringing bell would easily be heard. It obviously appeared to be a minor miracle to the witnessing students.

Another thrilling, but probably very rare, experience was for the students to witness the operation of a small steam engine. As water was changed to steam, steam into angular power, and angular power transferred into circular motion, the minds of the children were carried to that famous motive power, the steam locomotive. This engine helped them to understand that steam power was a tireless performer, and that eventually it would replace the horsepower with which they were so familiar in their daily lives on the farm.

The weight of air also was the base of another experiment within the grasp of the average student. The procedure was to weigh a container filled with air, and after the air was pumped out, weigh it again. A slight loss of weight was very evident. Air pumps could be bought costing from eight to one hundred dollars. Equipment such as this required a closed storage facility; otherwise, it would be constantly covered with dust and if not out of the way, could easily be damaged in the hustle and bustle of the classroom.

Scientific phenomena could be further demonstrated in an area known as hydrostatics. The simplest device demonstrated a fact which was bandied around in my General Science course in high school, namely, that water seeks its own level. This fact was so ably impressed upon us that when a student asked another one where he had been the night before (without knowing the precise answer), the respondent wisely repeated, "Water seeks its own level." I don't recall the mechanical device used to demonstrate this fact, but I do recall that the city's reserve supply of water was pumped into a high reservoir so that water would rise to the highest faucet located in the city.

The apparatus used to demonstrate this phenomena in the one-room schools of the nineteenth century consisted of a glass funnel mounted on a tube on which other forms were attached, such as a curved glass tube, a coil of glass, and a tapered glass container. When water was poured into the glass funnel, the water flowed through the glass tube to the other units and rose to the same level as in the funnel. The different shaped attachments were used to show that the shape of a vessel had no bearing on the performance of the experiment.

Another experiment with water was the operation of an Archimedes Screw. This pump consisted of a central core with the bottom end submerged in water. As the tube was turned, water rose to the top opening of the tube, apparently defying gravity. Although the writer has never seen such a contrivance in America, he did see plastic (of all things) examples displayed in a European trade fair in Holland.

Finally, some apparatus was used to make my dreaded course of physiology a meaningful experience to students of the one-room school. The most common object to assist in teaching the subject was a skull which had the lower jaw attached with a hinge, showing how the act of eating occurred.

An apparatus described in *Pennsylvania School Architecture* showed the function of the eye and its relation to concave and convex lens. Some apparatus showed the construction of the eye and another showed the effect of light as it fell on an eye through a lens. A demonstration of these objects helped Johnny to know why he could not see well through his grandpa's glasses. In those days, Grandpa got his spectacles by going to a store which had a variety of glasses, through which he could sort until he got the best pair for his eyes.

In order to encourage teachers to buy such equipment, some directions were given about its storage. It was recommended that a cabinet with panels of glass be provided, mounted on a firm foundation, probably the floor or a table top, the doors to be furnished with a lock to secure them from malicious meddling. The shelves should be provided with supports which could be moved to accommodate different sizes of equipment. The cabinet should be stored in the library if there was one; otherwise it should be placed where it was easily accessible. The teacher should have ready access to the apparatus so that there would be no reason not to use it.

The use of this apparatus obviously depended on the teacher's ability and willingness to put forth the extra effort required. In the first half of the nineteenth century there were few, if any, educational facilities for the training of teachers. By mid-century there were some higher institutions specializing in the training of teachers and, presumably, they would instruct teachers in the use of mechanical apparatus. As a student in a one-room school, I can easily imagine the interest students would have had in such presentations. Unfortunately, in my school there were none.

Desks designed for the seating of three or four students were roughly made and uncomfortable for sitting. The cast iron stove was an improvement over the fireplace used in many early schools. Courtesy: Old Time Schools and School Books.

 8

Desks and Chairs

Early school buildings, as has been pointed out, were roughly built, frequently of logs, and the fittings had a similar cast. The desks were made of thick slabs of wood, hewn on three sides, but planed smooth on the top on which writing was done. Benches were made of split logs with only one surface made smooth, the bottom side being the natural "round" of the tree from which the benches were made. Desks and benches were mounted on splayed legs, which were let into auger holes bored from the bottom and hopefully did not come through to the top. The benches had no backs.

It is a sad commentary that young children had to sit on such benches with virtually nothing to do to keep them busy. They had

neither slates nor books and received only a little attention from the teacher when he was not occupied disciplining the older students and drilling them in their work. The desks and benches were designed to seat ten students, and if scholars near the center wanted to get out, the easiest way was to climb over their desks. Of course, teachers were unable to get near inner students to give them individual attention. Such desks lacked ink pots and grooves for pencils in the earliest times, for neither was available.

One situation was described by Horace Mann in a report as follows:

In others, again long tables are prepared at which scholars sat face to face, like large companies at dinner. In others the seats are arranged on the sides of the room, the walls of the house forming the backs of the seats, and the scholars sit at desks facing inward, while in others, the desks are attached to the walls and the scholars face outward.

Such facilities were obviously built by the craftsmen who built the buildings. The builders continued to make the furniture, even when newer styles of desks and benches were made. the teacher's facility was a tall podium-like structure with a slanting top. The whole assembly was mounted on a small platform, which later turned into a raised platform the entire width of the schoolroom. This desk also served as a depository for confiscated tops, pocket knives, balls, and the like, becoming, in fact, a curiosity shop.

Later in the eighteenth century, benches were made of planed wood. There was a shelf under the desk top for books and lunches, the solid sides reaching from the top of the desk to the floor. These benches were also made of planed wood and were backless. Neither the desks nor the benches were attached to the floor, and pandemonium existed when the entire school shuffled their benches when arriving or leaving.

One contemporary authority about desks mentions that they were slanted toward the student, while in the outside world virtually all writing was done on a horizontal surface. The dichotomy of this situation was not resolved, and desks slanted for at least another hundred years.

The next step was to have the desk supported by the back of the bench in front of it. The entire unit continued to be made of boards by carpenters, and it was of necessity fastened to the floor; otherwise, when a scholar moved in his seat he would shake the desk to which his seat was attached. All parts were painted except the top of the desk and the bench. This arrangement allowed the desks to be made smooth after disfigurement from natural causes or the carvings of mischievous students.

The capacity of these benches ranged from ten to twelve students. Rarely was a seat built to accommodate only one student. It should be pointed out that boys and girls did not occupy one seat. As a matter of fact, the girls were segregated to one side of the room, the boys to the other. The benches continued to be too high for most of the students. This description is given in *Old Time Schools and School Books:*

The little scholars were most of the time "busy" keeping still. The backless benches they occupied were commonly too high for them, leaving their feet dangling in midair. Of course, they would get to knocking the shins of one another, a wiffet of laughter would escape, and the noise would increase until it attracted the attention of the master. Then down would come the pedagogue's ferrule on his desk with a clap that sent shivers through the little learners' hearts to think how it would have felt had it fallen somewhere else. "Silence," commanded the master, and he gave them a look that swept them into utter stillness.

By 1849, in *School Architecture*, a number of improved desks and chairs were illustrated, which were apparently recommended and used in the one-room schoolhouses. One set consisted of an attractive table replacing the earlier shelf-type desk. This table was mounted on four tapering legs. The unit was designed for two students and had two individual chairs made of wood, but was screwed to a cast iron stanchion (base).

An attractive feature of these chairs was the fact that they could be turned so that students could easily approach or leave. The back seems to have been less satisfactory, for it struck the scholar in the small of the back. These were called "Mott's patent revolving cast iron chairs."

The same chair continued to be used with the next style of desk, which had a shelf for books and was attached to a cast iron open grilled base which, like the base of the chair, was fastened to the floor. The chairs were made in four sizes, listed as follows:

No. 1 is 10 inches high and requires a desk 17 inches.

No. 2 is 12 inches high and requires a desk 19 1/2 inches.

No. 3 is 14 inches high and requires a desk 22 inches.

No. 4 is 16 inches high and requires a desk 24 inches.

The most sophisticated design consisted of a desk which had a slanting top with an ink pot and facility for pen and pencil, a shelf for books, and a chair mounted on an open-grilled cast iron support. Both the desk and the chair were fastened to the floor.

Contemporary with the last style was another which was highly recommended in furnishing a one-room schoolhouse. It was described as follows:

The end-pieces, or supports, both of the desk and the chair, are of cast iron, and the woodwork is attached with screws. They are made in eight sizes, giving a seat from ten to seventeen, and a desk at the edge next to the scholar from seventeen to twenty-six inches.

An assembly like this was used in my one-room schoolhouse and the only difference was that the seat was hinged and could be raised or lowered as dictated by the movements of the scholar. An added feature of my desk was that the wooden parts were made of alternating narrow boards of walnut and maple woods, which made a very striking appearance in the schoolroom. Occasionally one of these units turns up at a local antique shop in the York/Lancaster, Pennsylvania, region.

Most nearly like modern schoolroom furniture were some chairs designed for the Boston primary schools. One pattern was a chair with a shelf under the seat for the storage of books and a slate. The second pattern differed from the first in having a rack on the back of the chair for storage. The third pattern has a rack at the side of the chair instead of at the back. The price of these chairs was fifty cents for those with the shelf, and sixty-five for those with a rack.

Description of these presumably modern desks must have been the best of all, the way they were arranged in a classroom. The simplest way was to have them installed in rows with an aisle between every two rows. The desks separated by the aisles were designed for two students. Planners were very particular to have an aisle next to the exterior wall so that students did not sit close to the wall, which was cold in the winter. If an aisle for passage was not feasible, the desk would be placed at least six inches from the wall.

A novel way of arranging seats was an invention of Virgil Woodcock of Swanzey, New Hampshire, who received a patent for his plan. The editor of *Pennsylvania School Architecture* mentioned that he had never seen it used, but included a drawing of the plan for one who might want to use it. It consisted of staggering the desks, each chair opposite a desk in the adjoining row, with a narrow partition inserted between the desks. The plan was devised to save floor space and reduce students whispering to each other, which was easy to do if two were sitting side by side.

It is also mentioned, but not illustrated, that several chairs should be located on the platform of the schoolroom to seat visiting school committee members who wished to witness school activity. It was not an uncommon occurrence for school committee members to visit schools, not only for their own satisfaction that things were running well, but also for a chance to talk with the students. Speeches by committee members frequently mentioned the importance of an education and encouraged students to take care of the building, and lauded the teacher for the good job he was doing.

Not only were the desks of students improved, but similar progress was made in the construction of the teachers' desks. *Pennsylvania School Architecture* described this improvement.

In its place, convenient and handsome desks often grace the platforms. These not only ornament the schoolroom and add dignity to the teacher's position, but conduce to his efficiency and comfort by enabling him to have a place for all necessary aids to his calling, and to find them without confusion and delay.

The article said that the desk should have a level table-like surface on the top, not less than two feet wide by five feet long, with a ledge no higher than two or three inches at each end and back, and a movable inclined surface for writing, if desired. This was in line with earlier comments about writing on a level or slanting surface if the teacher wanted one. The desk shown had the entire top surface of the desk slightly inclined, with a pad of some sort placed in the middle of the top.

In comparison to the rest of the schoolroom furnishings, the teachers' desks illustrated seem very elegant. They had two piers or drawers, or one pier of drawers, and the other section had a door for the storage of large objects. One desk had a long drawer in the middle under

A design for a teacher's desk.
Courtesy: Pennsylvania School Architecture.

the top for the storage of big pieces of paper or maps. These desks looked like an antique "partner's" desk, with provision for one person to sit on each side of the desk, and have similar drawer facilities.

Obviously, all districts did not have desks of this type; some had less pretentious desks, and in some cases, the teacher had to get along with a table with one or two drawers. The teacher did have to have some space for the roll book, which seems to have been introduced soon after 1850 in some districts. In these books the daily attendance of the students was kept, and its contents were finally compared with similar accounts kept by the superintendent or principal. Such books were used as late as the early twentieth century, and the writer had the unhappy experience one year of having his accounts not perfectly similar to those of the principal. It was very hard to "forge" the contents and many hours were spent trying to have the figures come out right.

Finally, the teacher was to be supplied with a chair comparable in style to the desk. In the survey mentioned earlier, a chair was illustrated resembling a twentieth-century bar-room style. The chair had a cushion and the writer commented, "The cushion will do no harm if not used too much." The dignity and fine appearance was not in lieu of a poor teacher. The chair could not compensate for any inability the teacher might have. It was pointed out that as a general rule, the moving instructor was the best instructor.

9

Rules and Regulations

In appraising the high caliber of the products of the one-room schoolhouse, one is met with a very puzzling situation. It is very obvious the quality of the schoolhouse had little to do with the results. It has been pointed out that schoolhouses were shabby and in many cases falling apart. They were poorly heated and ventilated, and the source of light was often bad. the books were old and outdated in most cases, and originally had little to offer beyond the bare fundamentals of the subject. However, a moralist would point out that moral truths were to be found on virtually every page of a "reader," and, hopefully, they made a strong impression on the young scholars.

It might also be pointed out that teachers were untrained for their profession; however, it is very likely that many became good teachers. In the eighteenth century, many were educated in Europe and had a good background for their work in America. In the nineteenth century, many had no preparation for their profession beyond an extra year or two in the schools in which they finally taught.

In many cases the master was a minister who opened and closed the school day with a prayer, and was steadfast in his purpose to have the children read the Bible. It might be pointed out that often he was a stern taskmaster. He ruled his crowd with a ferrule (ruler) and a rod. Modern educators take a dim view of the use of such implements in the classroom, but today police roam the halls of schools in the big cities.

Maybe the procedure of writing at recess time five hundred times, "I have behaved badly," had some positive effect on behavior. And, of course, there was the dunce cap which bad students wore while standing in the corner facing the wall of the schoolroom.

Finally, one comes to the following rules and regulations. Were they so impressed on the young minds of the students that they became a part of them while they were growing up? Certainly George Washington was a fine example of his rules of civility that he copied when he was a child. It might be mentioned here that he as well as Thomas Jefferson, James Madison, and James Monroe all went to a one-room schoolhouse.

My analysis of the situation is that the high performance of these one-room graduates can be attributed to the influence of their parents. Many of them were endowed with a high regard for the high principles which influenced the lives of students. In my case, at least, that was the situation, much as I hate to discredit my schooling in a one-room schoolhouse. Maybe a bigger jury would have a different answer.

RULES AND REGULATIONS IN A ONE-ROOM SCHOOLHOUSE

1. Boys shall not chew, smoke tobacco, nor spit on the floor.
2. Girls shall not use snuff.
3. Fires should be started by leaving one inch of ashes, then proceed to build the fire. Place one stick on each side. In the space between them, place the kindling wood, and above it the small wood somewhat crosswise; then, set fire to the kindling and close the stove door. See that the draught is cleared of ashes or other obstructions, and that the dampers are properly adjusted (these are generally so arranged as to open the draught when the handle is parallel to the pipe). If materials have been laid according to the foregoing directions, the combustion will be free.
4. During the season of fires, the thermometer should be watched, and the ventilating flues, windows, doors, and stoves should be constantly attended, and every precaution taken to give as pure an atmosphere to the schoolroom as circumstances will allow.
5. The teacher should be careful to require all students to go out at recess, except those that can reasonably be excused on account of infirmity or sickness, and even these should be required to change their places

and exercise themselves by walking to and fro in the schoolroom.

6. A thermometric diary must be kept during the winter season, and the temperature of the room noted at the opening, middle, and close of the school day.

7. The window blinds and curtains should be so managed to exclude the direct rays of the sun, and kept open or shut accordingly.

8. At all seasons, at the close of the school day, all the doors and windows should be opened for a few minutes in order that pure atmosphere can be admitted and retained during the noontime recess, or at night.

9. For a large room, or one department of a public school building, six brooms will be found sufficient to be in use. When half worn out, they will serve for sweeping the yard, and when well worn down in that service, they will be useful for scrubbing with water or sand; and, if properly used by the sweepers, will be evenly worn to the last.

10. The dirt, when taken up, should be carried into the middle of the street.

11. In outdoor sweeping, the sweepers should operate in ranks, and sweeping from the windward.

12. The broom should rest square on the floor, and with the motion of raking hay, should be drawn toward the sweeper without flirting it outwards or upwards, which raises unnecessary dust, and wears the broom unevenly.

13. The pupil should stand erect—his heels together, toes turned outward, and his eyes directed to the face of the person speaking to him.

14. Boys and girls are required to be punctual at school.

15. They should scrape their feet on the scraper, and wipe them on every mat they pass over on their way to the hall.

16. To bow gracefully and respectfully on entering and leaving the hall (schoolroom), and any recitation when a teacher is present.

17. Keep their persons, clothes, and shoes clean.

18. To give notice of all books, slates, etc., missing.

19. Take their place on entering the hall.

20. To make no unnecessary noise within the walls of the building at any time, day or night.

21. To carry and bring their books in a satchel.

22. To study lessons at home, except when inconvenient to the family. In such cases bring a certificate of the fact in writing.

23. To present a pen by the feathered end, a knife by its handle, a book the right side upward to read by the person receiving it.

24. To bring notes of absence dated and signed by the person authorized to do so, stating the duration of the absence. Also, notes for tardiness and for occasions when students are wanted at home before the regular hour of dismissal.

25. To deposit in desks all books (except writing books), slates, pencils, rulers, etc., before dismissal.

26. To pick up hats, caps, pens, slips, books, etc., found on the floor and put them to their appropriate places.

27. Show two fingers when a pen is wanted. (?)

28. Write all requests on slates and wait until called.

29. Put all refuse paper, stumps of pens, etc., in the dust box.

30. Be particularly vigilant when no teacher is in the hall.

31. To fill all vacant time with ciphering as a general occupation, and to give notice to the teacher before dismissal, in case of omitting the exercise wholly on any day.

32. To promote as far as possible the happiness, comfort, and improvement of others.

33. Be accountable for the condition of the floor nearest their own desk.

34. To raise the hand as a request to speak across the hall or any recitation room.

35. Close desk and fasten them before leaving school.

36. To stand while speaking to the teacher.

37. To follow every classmate while reading, and correct all errors discovered in pronunciation, emphasis, or inflection.

38. Rest the body on the left arm while spelling, and keep eyes directed toward their own slate.

39. Point the finger of the left hand at each letter or figure of the slip or the copy while writing, and the feather of the pen towards the right shoulder.

40. Sit erectly against the back of the chairs during the singing lessons, and direct their attention to the instructor.

41. Keep all books clean and the contents of desks neatly arranged.

42. Don't read any book in school without the teacher's knowledge.

43. Don't throw pens, paper, or anything whatever on the floor or out the window or door.
44. Boys are forbidden to buy or sell, borrow or lend, give, take, or exchange anything, except fruit or other eatable without the teacher's permission.
45. Go out to play when he has had a deviation.
46. A boy should not climb any fence, railing, ladder, etc., about the schoolhouse.
47. Students are not allowed to mark, cut, scratch, chalk, or otherwise disfigure, injure, or defile any portion of the building, or anything connected with it.
48. No one is allowed to take out an ink stand, meddle with the contents of another's desk, or unnecessarily open or shut his own.
49. Students should not write without using a card and wiper.
50. Students should not quit school without having finished his copy.
51. No one is allowed to study home lessons during school hours.
52. Scholars should not leave the schoolroom without proper leave.
53. Scholars should not run or noisily go from one room to another, or through the entries.
54. Students are not allowed to visit office, furnace room, or any closet or teacher's room without a written permit.
55. No one should nickname anyone.
56. Eating and drinking in school is not allowed.
57. Students should not play at *Paw paw* anywhere, or any game within the building.
58. Don't carry your pen on your ear.
59. Don't remove class lists from their depositories.
60. Don't use a knife, except on conditions prescribed.
61. Don't leave whittlings or other rubbish on the playground, on the sidewalk, or around the building.
62. No one is to use profane or indelicate language.
63. Don't waste school hours by unnecessary talking, laughing, playing, idling, standing up, turning around, teasing, or otherwise calling the attention of another boy.
64. Scholars should not throw stones, snowballs, or other missiles about the neighborhood of the school.
65. Don't bring bats, hockey sticks, bows and arrows, or other dangerous playthings to school.
66. Don't visit a privy in company with anyone.
67. Don't strike, push, or otherwise annoy associates.
68. Hooks for hanging caps should be provided with as much certainty as seats to sit on.
69. It is desirable to remove students from temptations.
70. The claims of cleanliness are too commanding to be resisted and should ever be maintained.
71. Making scholars committeemen must have a very good effect on the operation of the schoolroom.
72. Children often infringe school regulations, and much is to be overlooked in them when at a very tender age.
73. A hypocrite may be courteous, but hypocrisy in a child is inexpressibly loathsome.
74. A sensibility to the beautiful needs to be cultivated among us (adults), and may easily be done with the young if a proper and sincere value be placed upon it by yourselves, and the children see that our admiration is a reality.
75. Children should be taught to take leave of their parents and friends on going to school, and to offer the friendly salute and kind inquiry on returning home.
76. Choose good companions and fly from the bad.
77. Speaking the truth is the most substantial foundation of moral character.
78. Each desk should be furnished with a slate, pencil holder, and sponge. A slate to every scholar child, young or old, is of utmost importance.
79. The cardinal points of the compass should be painted on the ceiling of the schoolroom and associated by frequent references of the teacher, with the parts of the heavens in which the sun rises and sets.
80. Every schoolhouse should have its own well with suitable arrangements for drink, and for the cleanliness of the pupils.
81. No personal notes should be interchanged between male and female members of the school.
82. Pupils should not throw wipers at each other.
83. Religious and secular ethics are important subjects to school students.
84. Tall trees should partially shade the school grounds.
85. It is very desirable that the teacher's desk be in the north direction so that students' desks will face them.

86. Books, apparatus, and collections should always be protected by doors.

87. There should be a wood box or closet large enough to hold several cords of wood.

88. All projections in the walls, as well as pillars to support the roof, ought to be avoided for they interfere with the arrangement within the schoolroom.

89. The teacher should give general instruction from the platform in the front of the schoolroom and hear each class separately.

90. The benches for class recitation should not be fastened to the floor, but be movable when circumstances call for such action.

91. Provision might be made for the teacher's residence in the schoolhouse and thus be a part of the teacher's compensation.

92. It is absolutely essential for pupils to receive physical training, as well as training in the importance of kindness and honesty.

93. Female students should not be confined to a sitting posture with but a scanty allowance for robust and active exercises which impart power to the muscular system and invigorate the general health.

94. Chairs should vary in height so the feet of all students rest securely on the floor.

95. A good assortment of apparatus should be available to illustrate all the important principles of Natural Philosophy, Chemistry, and Human Physiology.

96. Fill the water basins every morning and wash them twice a week.

97. Cabinets for minerals and other objects of Natural History should be provided.

98. The platform on which the teacher's desk is placed should be of sufficient height to give the teacher full view of the whole school.

99. There should be one closet assigned for the teacher's private use.

100. A cellar might be paved with bricks and serve as a play room in inclement weather.

101. Has anything been missed?